COULD IT HAPPEN HERE?

Canada in the Age of Trump and Brexit

MICHAEL ADAMS

Published by Simon & Schuster

New York London Toronto Sydney New Delhi

SIMON &
SCHUSTER
CANADA

Simon & Schuster Canada
A Division of Simon & Schuster, Inc.
166 King Street East, Suite 300
Toronto, Ontario M5A 1J3

This Simon & Schuster Canada edition September 2017

SIMON & SCHUSTER CANADA and colophon are registered trademarks of
Simon & Schuster, Inc.

For information about special discounts for bulk purchases, please contact
Simon & Schuster Special Sales at 1-800-268-3216 or CustomerService@
simonandschuster.ca.

Library & Archives Canada Catalog-in-Publication

Adams, Michael, 1946 Sept. 29–, author
   Could it happen here? / Michael Adams.
   Issued in print and electronic formats.
   ISBN 978-1-5011-7742-2- (hardcover).—ISBN 978-1-5011-7744-6 (ebook)
      1. Social surveys—Canada. 2. Social prediction—Canada.
   3. Populism—Canada—Forecasting. 4. Social values—Canada.
   5. Demographic surveys—Canada. 6. Canada—Economic
   conditions—21st century. I. Title.
   HN110.Z9S67 2017   303.4971   C2017-902218-0
                                               C2017-902219-9

Manufactured in the United States of America

10 9 8 7 6 5 4 3 2 1

ISBN 978-1-5011-7742-2
ISBN 978-1-5011-7744-6 (ebook)

To Thuy Thi Nguyen

Contents

Preface

I have spent much of my adult life studying Canadian exceptionalism from the perspective of survey research, drawing on Environics's extensive archive of polling of values, attitudes and opinions going all the way back to the mid-1970s. My curiosity about my own country led me to wonder how Canadians differed from our cousins in the United States and Europe. This curiosity inspired me to publish my first book, in 1997, *Sex in the Snow: The Surprising Revolution in Canadian Social Values*. That book drew on annual social values surveys conducted in Canada since 1983 and a couple of surveys conducted in the U.S. in 1992 and 1996, presidential election years. *Sex in the Snow* documented the evolution of Canadian social values from deference to authority to questioning authority, from patriarchy to gender equality, from fear and judgment of others to openness to others, from deferred gratification to immediate gratification, from the consumption of material symbols of status and success to a postmaterial orientation to learning and experience seeking, and from a reliance on religious authority for meaning to a more philosophical and personal spiritual quest.

Fire and Ice: The United States, Canada and the Myth of Converging Values was published in 2003. That book was firmly focused on the revolutionary and counterrevolutionary cousins in North America. It was based on our annual Canadian survey program up to 2000 and the relatively newer U.S. program, drawing on the surveys conducted in 1992 and 1996, as well as a third in 2000. *Fire and Ice* demonstrated, at least to my satisfaction, that Canadian and American social values were diverging—not converging as both elites and the Canadian public at large assumed. Among other surprising findings that book reported was a growing orientation to patriarchy in the United States. In 1992, 42 per cent of Americans agreed that "the father of the family must be master in his own house"; the proportion had risen to 48 per cent by 2000 as Americans were about to choose Bill Clinton's successor, George W. Bush. In Canada, the proportion over that eight-year period had dropped from 26 per cent to 18 per cent.

Jump forwards a decade and a half, and the world around us seems very different from the world of the 1990s documented in my early books. Our international scene is convulsed by terrorism, thousands of refugees are making perilous flights from war and oppression, and populist political uprisings are shocking experts and unnerving moderates of all persuasions. Canada appears placid, at least on its surface. As the U.S., Britain and other societies retrench, the international media have taken notice of Canada's apparent calm. After nearly two years in power, Canada's centrist Liberal government continues to enjoy majority approval, suggesting an electorate not as bitterly split as those elsewhere. Open on immigration, rational on climate, and unapologetic on gender equity, the Trudeau Liberals cleave to principles that seemed relatively safe in many Western societies only a few years ago but are under threat in many places today.

As skeptics point out, however, Brexit and a Trump presidency were unthinkable until they happened, and Canada is not immune to the forces of populism, social fracture and backlash. A massacre at a Quebec City mosque offered a grim window onto an extremist subculture. At least two Conservative leadership candidates drew inspiration from the Trump worldview. Opinion polls show anxiety among Canadians about the cultural integration of newcomers.

The evening of November 8, 2016, was my tipping point. As Pennsylvania, Michigan and Wisconsin appeared set to give Donald Trump his electoral college victory, I knew I had to revisit the questions that had inspired my earlier efforts to share our social-values research with Canadian readers. What was the survey data saying? Were we at risk of coming down with the malaise affecting other Western democracies? The next day I rushed into the office to ask for the results of the survey of eight thousand Americans and four thousand Canadians that had just come out of the field. The question on my mind was one that many Canadians have asked since then—in the media, at the bar and around the dinner table: *Could it happen here?* This book is my answer.

Could It Happen Here?

When Conservative MP Kellie Leitch launched her long-shot, and ultimately unsuccessful, bid to replace Stephen Harper as party leader, she was making a bet. Leitch positioned herself as a clarion for those Canadians who felt alienated and angry about high levels of immigration from non-European, non-Christian countries, as well as an influx of refugees from war-ravaged Syria. It was an overt appeal to the sort of nationalist populism that has gripped much of the West in the past two or three years. For a time, Leitch's views garnered a lot of attention, and it even looked like she could emerge as the winner of the epic campaign to succeed Harper.

As her showpiece platform plank, Leitch—a physician from Creemore, a town north of Orangeville, Ontario—pledged that all newcomers and visitors would have to take a "Canadian values" test as a condition of entry. A few other candidates, including former immigration minister Chris Alexander, had similar positioning, while the early presumed front-runner, reality TV star Kevin O'Leary, offered himself up as a populist in the mould of Donald Trump.

While Leitch insisted her scheme wasn't meant to serve as a racist dog whistle for white, rural and disaffected voters (many of whom approved of the sorts of messages coming from Donald Trump), it nonetheless looked like an obvious sequel to her advocacy for the Harper-era "Barbaric Cultural Practices" hotline,[1] a much-ridiculed proposal introduced as legislation by Alexander in June 2015.[2] Ostensibly meant to protect girls and women, the law and the accompanying government hotline were assailed by critics and opposition parties as a way for the government to slyly woo voters unsettled by immigrants and cultures that seemed too, well, "foreign." Leitch's values test seemed to be a tidied-up version of those earlier signals.

To many observers of the Harper government, such moves—combined with policies such as withholding government-funded health services for asylum seekers, a historically parsimonious pose on admitting Syrian refugees, bans on niqabs for public servants,[3] legislation that threatened to strip Canadian citizenship from immigrants convicted of crimes[4] and tougher voter registration rules—represented a clear pivot away from the Conservatives' earlier open views on immigrant constituencies.

From the first days of Harper's term as prime minister, the Conservatives appeared to be intent on forging strong political links with ethnocultural groups whose members have traditionally aligned themselves with the Liberal Party. Harper's view, supported by the party's own polling and other public opinion research, was that many newcomers harboured socially conservative values and gravitated to a more austere vision of government. In short, many immigrants were natural Conservative voters; the party just had to let them know it.

The prime minister dispatched a senior minister, Jason Kenney, a former Reform Party MP and present leader of Alberta's Progressive Conservatives, to forge connections with a wide range of ethnocultural communities. Kenney had for years made a point of visiting festivals, temples and ceremonies, and generally dispelling the stubborn idea that the Conservative Party of Canada was mainly the preserve of white, rural, small-town Canadians, voters typically seen as the party's "base."

For a time, the strategy bore fruit, and it helped propel the party to a majority—tellingly, the first majority in the country's history without a substantial number of seats in Quebec. During the 2011 federal election, the Harper Conservatives, having survived two terms as a minority government as well as the brutal recession of 2009, made impressive inroads into ridings with large or even dominant newcomer or immigrant communities. Those regions spanned the country, from south Vancouver to the post–World War II inner suburbs of the City of Toronto, the sturdiest of Liberal bastions, and much of the Maritimes.[5] Whatever the motives and political calculations behind the strategy, the Conservative game plan was clear proof that the road to majority status in Canada ran directly through the heart of those urban and suburban neighbourhoods that exemplify the new Canada—a country more positively invested in immigration than almost any other developed economy in the world.

Immigrants, as of late 2016, accounted for 22.1 per cent of Canada's population, a proportion that has increased steadily for the past six decades. The concentration is even greater in Canada's largest cities. Foreign-born residents account for almost half the population of Greater Toronto, a metric that makes the country's largest metropolis the most diverse urban region in the world, according to a 2016 study conducted by BBC Radio.[6] Those immigrants now come overwhelmingly from outside Europe, with eight in ten arriving from Asia, Africa, Latin America and the Caribbean. Fully a fifth of Canada's residents are now members of a visible minority group.

What's more, the proportion of foreign-born residents in Canada has long exceeded that of the other wealthy immigrant-receiving nations, including the United States (13 per cent as of 2010), the United Kingdom (12.7 per cent in 2011[7]), Germany (13 per cent), and France (11.7 per cent as of 2010). Only a handful of countries—among them Australia, Switzerland and New Zealand—have more international populations.

Given Canada's demographic realities, the Harper government's shift in the year or so leading up to the 2015 federal election was surprising and, in hindsight, self-destructive. Having spent years trying to prove to newcomer communities that they were different than earlier generations of small-*c* conservative politicians, the Tories launched policy after policy that seemed to demonstrate precisely the opposite: that refugees didn't deserve health care until their cases had been adjudicated (the law was declared unconstitutional by the Supreme Court); that citizens needed to jump over higher hurdles to register to vote; and that some cultural habits could be called out by self-appointed citizen-judges as "barbaric."

Postmortem analyses, in fact, concluded that the government's move to rescind the citizenship of Zakaria Amara (convicted in 2010 of terrorist activities) right in the midst of the 2015 federal election proved to be a game-changing moment, mobilizing thousands of Muslim-Canadian voters against the Conservatives.[8] As some Tories insisted in the aftermath of their defeat, they'd gotten the policy right but the tone wrong.

THERE WAS SOMETHING perplexing about Leitch's gambit to win the leadership by adopting a stance that had already proved to be a grave miscalculation during the 2015 election campaign. In fact, when the Conservatives finally cast their votes for a new leader in late May 2017, Leitch endured a resounding defeat—she never got more than 8 per cent of the votes cast and had to drop off the ballot midway through the process of winnowing the field. Conservatives instead coalesced behind Andrew Scheer's cheerful social conservatism and Maxime Bernier's radical libertarianism, with neither hitching his programs to the sort of populist politics that characterized Leitch's bid.

It is true that, despite generally world-leading positive attitudes towards immigrants and multiculturalism, there is evidence that Canadians do, in fact, worry about whether newcomers are integrating successfully into Canadian society and whether they're adopting "Canadian values," however respondents interpret that phrase.

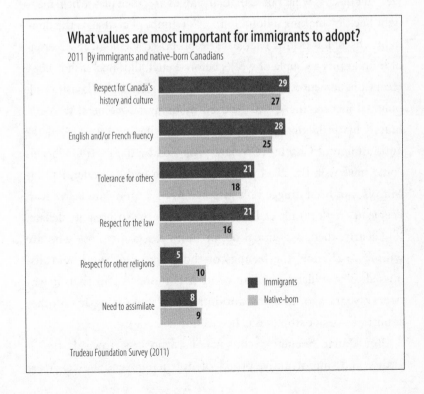

What values are most important for immigrants to adopt?

2011 By immigrants and native-born Canadians

	Immigrants	Native-born
Respect for Canada's history and culture	29	27
English and/or French fluency	28	25
Tolerance for others	21	18
Respect for the law	21	16
Respect for other religions	5	10
Need to assimilate	8	9

Trudeau Foundation Survey (2011)

A second concern that has become entangled with our immigrant-integration conversation is the fear of terrorism. However unhelpful the conflation of these two issues, they are nevertheless mingled in the minds of many here and elsewhere. Even when a Canadian-born, Christian-raised man of European descent embarks on an attack in the name of ISIS, some see it as a problem that has come from "there" to "here" and from "them" to "us."

Recent years have also shown us that a backlash constituency does exist, alarmed by some aspects of living in a diverse society and affronted by the fact that they are not permitted to air their alarm without being accused of racism. It is no accident that Leitch's campaign literature had an aggrieved tone: "If you are tired of feeling like we can't discuss what our Canadian values are, then please help me to fight back by making a donation . . ." Trump, of course, is the dominant champion of this backlash; he proposed ideological screening of immigrants a couple of weeks before Leitch did. Backlash is not a recent phenomenon, either—Toronto mayor Rob Ford, lavish in his political incorrectness, was beloved by many newcomers, who embraced his little-guy-fighting-smug-liberal-elites narrative. And the anti-immigrant Charter of Values proposed by the Parti Québécois could have won the 2014 provincial election had its leader, Pauline Marois, not been dragged off message by star candidate Pierre Karl Péladeau's high-profile calls for the revival of the sovereignty debate.

Clearly, then, a political opportunity exists for those who are willing to channel the feelings of those who feel angry and dismissed. The wider Canadian context is more fearful than it was twenty years ago, and the anti-immigrant messaging from other countries doesn't stop at our borders.

But Canada remains conspicuously positive towards immigrants and, importantly, proud of not being xenophobic. Most

Canadians—especially immigrants—feel pride in their country. One of the things many Canadians are most proud of is a belief that different kinds of people can live here in harmony, and that immigrants and their children—who together now account for 40 per cent of the country's population—are just as good citizens as anyone born here, if not better.

For all that, Leitch's proposed values test for newcomers raised an intriguing question: In a country that increasingly defines itself by its ethnocultural diversity and tends to reject muscular displays of patriotic fervour, what would those common-denominator values even look like? What are Canada's core values?

Our surveys show clearly that we continue to value good government, our public health-care system, multiculturalism and diversity, personal safety and civic participation. But our research also illustrates that Canadian values tilt heavily in the direction of a progressive vision of society. We rank gender equality as our greatest aspirational value and quickly embraced gay marriage. But we also respect a variety of religions, including socially conservative ones, provided they abide by the rule of law. Over 90 per cent of Canadians support or strongly support a social safety net to help those confronting financial tribulations, poverty or just bad luck. By contrast, only a little more than half agree that low taxes are a paramount concern. Immigrants, moreover, tend to identify similar values as Canadians who were born here.

Moreover, public opinion research in Canada reveals a long, steady run of support for immigration as a positive force. Since the early 1990s, regularly conducted surveys have shown that a clear majority of Canadians, even in economic downturns, reject the notion that immigration levels are too high and that newcomers take jobs away from other Canadians.

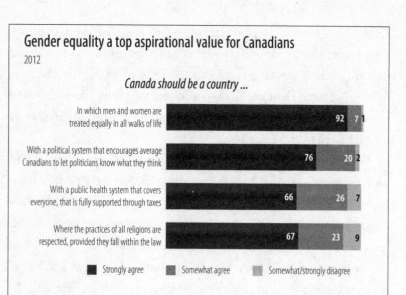

Gender equality a top aspirational value for Canadians
2012

Canada should be a country ...

Environics Institute: Trudeau Foundation Survey (2012)

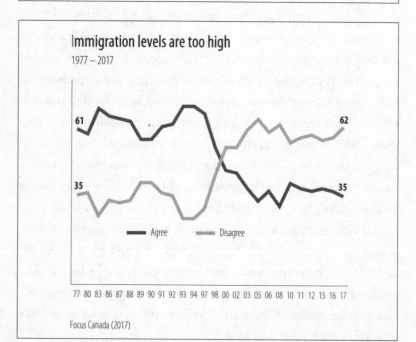

Immigration levels are too high
1977 – 2017

Focus Canada (2017)

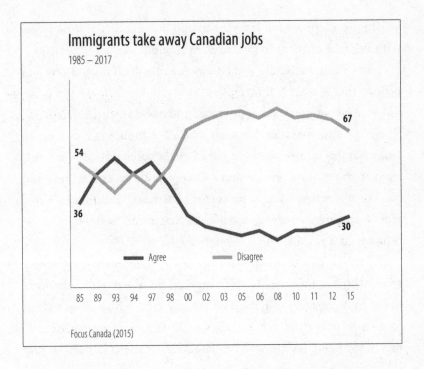

Immigrants take away Canadian jobs
1985 – 2017

54

36

67

30

Agree   Disagree

85 89 93 94 97 98 00 02 03 05 06 08 10 11 12 15

Focus Canada (2015)

But if that's the case, why are so many Canadians watching events in Donald Trump's America with such a deep sense of trepidation?

"Could *it*," we ask ourselves in dog parks, at dinner parties, or in the stands of local hockey arenas, "happen *here*?" Will we "catch Trumpism," that storm of angry, isolationist and frequently nativist populism that has swept through not only the United States but also the United Kingdom in the Brexit era, Germany, France, Hungary, Poland and even redoubts of progressivism like the Netherlands?

There *are* Canadians who want "it"—or some version of "it"—to happen here. Jean-François Lisée won the Parti Québécois leadership in the fall of 2016 by promising to reduce immigration and ban the burka in public. Even the ruling Quebec Liberals held hearings on a proposed law that would make it illegal for anyone with her face covered to give or obtain public services.[9]

Some Canadians have lost confidence in federal institutions and believe that we are admitting too many refugees from the Muslim-majority countries that produce fundamentalists and terrorists. There are clear parallels between readers of Breitbart News in the United States and devotees of Ezra Levant's Rebel Media, a hard-right Internet news service that calls out political correctness and baits progressives. ("Racist university apartheid," headlines a Rebel report on postsecondary institutions that offer "scholarships for refugees, not whites."[10])

Analysts love to point out that many Canadians—especially those who live in large, dense cities with diverse populations—are living in a progressive bubble or fantasy land which allows them to assume that their benign views of newcomers, trans people or mixed-race couples are widely shared across society, when in fact many parts of Canada have little exposure to social diversity and are less favourably disposed to it.

There are dangers associated with this disconnect. In March 2017, veteran political journalist Michael Valpy noted that "persistent and deepening" economic pessimism was inflected with racism and xenophobia. He used the findings from an EKOS poll to offer up a stern reminder about how American pollsters and pundits so dramatically misread the American mood in 2016. Valpy noted that the political and media establishment should be wary of ignoring populist anger among those Canadians, especially on the right, who express fear or resentment about how the country is run.

"Those supporters are real people—and there are a lot of them," Valpy wrote. "Dismissing them and their concerns, however crudely they may be stated at times—as the U.S. media did with Americans who flocked to Mr. Trump's standard—is frankly more likely to increase their numbers and more deeply entrench their anger and their (justifiable) sense of being held in contempt by the mainstream media and political establishment."[11]

It wasn't the first time that the assemblers and purveyors of conventional wisdom—columnists, political scientists, pundits, poll-aggregating analytics whizzes, etc.—had drastically misread the mood of an electorate and, by extension, society broadly.

In the City of Toronto, during the 2010 municipal election, long-standing observers of local politics underestimated the populist appeal of Rob Ford, a local councilor known for his red-faced outbursts and his habit of summoning senior bureaucrats to the homes of constituents seeking help for mundane problems. Though positioned as a hard-right, pro-car conservative who was going to slash spending and dismantle his predecessor's plans for a light rail network, Ford won big in the city's suburbs. He tapped into support from many immigrants and those who felt a left-leaning, downtown elite had produced a bloated, wasteful municipal government all too prone to cave in to public-sector union demands and strike actions. As Western University political scientist Zack Taylor noted in a 2011 postmortem, "Financially squeezed voters tended to support Ford."[12]

Five years later, the run-up to the Brexit referendum in the U.K. also revealed a yawning gap between the expectations of the chattering classes and the ultimate voting behaviour of the electorate. For most of the year preceding that June 2016 vote, dozens of polls put the "Remain" forces comfortably ahead of "Leave," although the numbers narrowed, briefly flip-flopped and eventually settled into a statistical tie in the days leading up to the ballot.[13]

Those tasked with reading the tea leaves offered up their analysis. "A high overall turnout will likely benefit Remain, as young

people and richer old folk are keener on the union, but a big turnout
is far from guaranteed," predicted *The Economist*, that most elite
of British publications, on the eve of the vote.[14] As it transpired,
the turnout was unexpectedly high, including among millennials
blamed heretofore for their complacency. But the Leave forces—led
by Nigel Farage and Boris Johnson—mobilized enough older Anglo-
Saxons to deliver the victory.

Given this turbulent international scene, how should Canadians reconcile the insistent and growing warnings about the rising tide of made-in-Canada populism and anti-Muslim sentiment
with our attitudes towards what has been happening in the U.S.
under Trump's presidency?

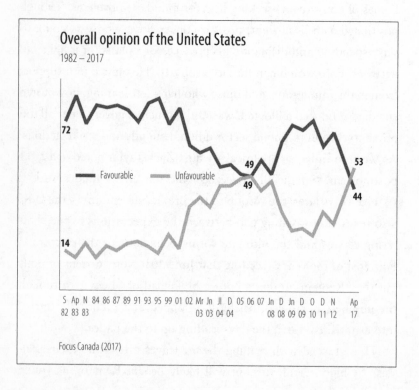

Overall opinion of the United States
1982 – 2017

72

49
49

53

44

14

— Favourable   — Unfavourable

S Ap N 84 86 87 89 91 93 95 99 01 02 Mr Jn Jl D 05 06 07 Jn D Jn D O D N   Ap
82 83 83   03 03 04 04   08 08 09 09 10 11 12   17

Focus Canada (2017)

It's no secret that many Canadians, all across the country, were broadly supportive of Trump's predecessor, Barack Obama, and there's little doubt that Justin Trudeau sought to make the most of the forty-fourth president's personal popularity north of the border.

Early in Trump's long-shot run, Canadian pollsters discovered that we didn't much care for the real estate developer–turned–reality TV show star. Long before he began making specific threats about import tariffs on Canadian energy, lumber and dairy, a 2015 survey found that only one in six Canadians liked Trump, and a similarly small proportion thought he'd be good for Canada.[15]

In the days leading up to the election, when Canadians were polled to see how they'd vote hypothetically in the U.S. race, Trump fared so poorly that more respondents reported they would back one of the third-party candidates, like the Green Party's Jill Stein, or abstain rather than cast a ballot for the blustery billionaire.

A few days after Trump's upset victory, a Forum poll published in *The Toronto Star* revealed that while four in ten of those surveyed didn't like Hillary Clinton, the vast majority were un-ambiguous in their views of the new commander-in-chief. No less than 80 per cent of the Canadian women surveyed disapproved of Trump, whose crude sexual talk and boasting about assaulting women captured on a live microphone seemed, for a while, to doom his campaign.

Only a third of Albertans favoured Trump, and that was by far the highest level of support in any Canadian province, despite his support for the controversial Keystone pipeline that would trans-port Alberta crude to U.S. refineries. As *The Toronto Star* reported, "53 per cent of Canadian voters said they were not at all satis-

fied with the outcome of the election, while 17 per cent said they
were not very satisfied. Fifty-five per cent of respondents agreed
that Trump as president would be bad for Canada, and 73 per cent
overall disapprove of him."[16]

Those attitudes haven't improved much after months of eye-popping political chaos in Washington, daily conspiracy theories,
surreal fights over fake news, and vague threats from the Trump
administration about import tariffs that could drag down the Canadian economy. The immigration and travel ban also brought
waves of stories about Canadians being refused entry into the U.S.,
as well as groups—from Girl Guides to school trips to academics—
opting not to risk a run-in at the border.

POLITICAL SENTIMENTS TRAVEL easily, like dandelion spores,
across borders, oceans and even linguistic divides. The angry
populist mood in the U.K. and the U.S. has emboldened anti-immigrant, isolationist politicians and right-wing parties in many
parts of Europe, and visa versa. Canadians are no more immune
to those trends than anyone else. We're in a moment when simmering populist discontent, which never really goes away, has
been given a voice and a standard-bearer and a whole lot of raw
energy that can be used to embolden disgruntled nativists and
recruit voters.

But those ideas land or take root in societies with their own
distinctive strengths and weaknesses, histories, geographies, demographics, economies and value systems. Some countries drawn
to xenophobic nationalism have generally happier citizens (e.g.,
Denmark and Switzerland[17]); others are home to angrier residents
who are attracted to authoritarian figures and tolerate inequality or
higher levels of violence (such as the U.S.).

Consequently, any discussion about whether "it" could happen here demands that we move beyond the churn of public opinion polls and partisan punditry, and look instead at underlying measures of civic or social health: Can we passionately debate issues of great public interest without lapsing into gridlock or discourse poisoned by accusations? Can we ground our debates in some kind of common understanding of the pertinent facts? Do we have faith in our democracy and shared institutions, or do we hanker to destroy them? Can we recognize "outsiders"—whether recent immigrants, refugees, trans folk, Muslims or anyone else—as individuals or do we see them as targets for hatred?

One important answer to this question is, "*Of course*, it can happen here!" You needn't look too far into the history books to find examples of societies that abruptly pivoted away from rights, democratic governance and religious tolerance. Sometimes, plain old bad luck intervenes and changes the course of the plot. But countries that have managed—either by intention or good fortune—to foster social resilience, reduce inequality and provide collective tax-supported government insurance against ill health or unemployment are more likely to be able to withstand the clarion calls from the Trumps of this world. Canada, as it turns out, is one such nation, although not the only one.

This isn't a smug assertion of Canadian exceptionalism so much as an acknowledgement of our own recent political history. After episodes of raucous populism, surging anti-immigrant sentiment and even the rise (and subsequent fall) of socially conservative governments in some western provinces, Canadians already know what "it" looks like. In some sense, parts of Canada have been there and done that. The appetite for that form of politics is limited. After all, there are less raucous ways to achieve peace, order and good government.

CHAPTER ONE

The Global Re-awakening of Xenophobic Populism

A hurricane.

That's perhaps the best word to describe the gusts of noisy, populist and anger-fueled nationalism that seem to be blowing from country to country in these fitful days, whipping up resentments many people thought had been safely buried in an increasingly remote past.

To some casual observers, the storm may have seemed to touch down first in the United Kingdom, with the shock of the 2016 Brexit referendum outcome. But it had already picked up momentum by then, drawing energy from ambient global anxiety about ISIS-sponsored terrorism; simmering post-2008 economic uncertainty in countries like Greece and Italy; a torrent of refugees pouring out of Africa and the Middle East; Vladimir Putin's unsettlingly aggressive expansionism; mounting climate change anxiety; and the escalating racial, political and economic tensions in the United States.

This unstable weather system has careened through parts of central and northern Europe, as well as France, Australia, Turkey, the Philippines and, of course, Donald Trump's America. Authoritarian, isolationist politics is in ascendancy. The president of the most powerful nation in the world congratulates dictators when they consolidate power and disparages journalists as "the most dishonest human beings on earth" and enemies of the people. In a world steeped in uncertainty, bellicose blame, it would seem, sells, and sells well.

The last time the world saw this kind of vertiginous global re-ordering was back in the 1980s with the implosion of the Soviet Bloc. That disintegration began with the Solidarity demonstrations led by a fearless labour leader working on the docks of Gdańsk and spread inexorably across Eastern Europe and the Soviet Union until the whole edifice collapsed with the dismantling of the Berlin Wall in November 1989. Ronald Reagan and Mikhail Gorbachev each did his part to accelerate the process, but those velvet revolutions were populist and notably peaceful affairs, driven by ordinary people who had had enough of Big Brother.

In the bewildered aftermath, a previously obscure American political scientist and economist, Francis Fukuyama, penned a polemical tome that declared victory for the forces of liberal democracy. *The End of History and the Last Man*, published in 1992, posited that, with the demise of the great collectivist experiments imposed by the heirs of Marx and Lenin, the world could transition rationally to a bright future of democracy, free trade, the rule of law and consumer goods for everyone, all in the service of global capitalism.

Critics disparaged his hypothesis, but there was much evidence to support Fukuyama's prognostication, at least early on. North America, Europe and a number of other regions of the globe had consolidated into free-trade blocs, a transformation that produced not only increased cross-border commerce and flow of investment capital, as the orthodox liberal economists had predicted, but also a growing movement of people in search of economic prosperity.

The links between China and the U.S., gingerly established in the 1970s by Richard Nixon's unexpected diplomatic skills, began to proliferate rapidly with the liberalization that followed the brutal state clampdowns during the June 1989 Tiananmen Square demonstrations.[1] Thanks to ever longer supply chains, just-in-time production and the outsourcing of vast tracts of the West's industrial base to Southeast Asia or *maquiladora* zones in Mexico, consumerism began to drive the global economy and, it appeared, bring new wealth to previously impoverished nations, like China and India. Despite speed bumps like the 1997 Asian financial/currency crisis, the predicted progress of globalization seemed to be proceeding apace, pushed along with increasing momentum by the global adoption of the Internet, the spread of wireless communication networks and e-commerce.

But not all was quiet on the Western front in the 1990s. The former Yugoslavia was ravaged by ethnic and sectarian strife as Serbs, Croats, Bosnians, Albanians and others found themselves engulfed in excruciating wars of ethnic cleansing. The explosion of violence reminded the world that the resentments that had led to the assassination of Archduke Franz Ferdinand and the initiation of World War I continued to pulse just beneath the surface of Tito's Communist dictatorship. The bloody revival of ancient animosities close to the heart of Europe hinted that history was not ready to release us from its grasp just yet.

Even more unexpectedly, another kind of history interrupted the story of globalization with an assault on mainland America, the first since the British, defending British North America (Canada), burned the White House during the War of 1812. Al Qaeda's attack on the World Trade Center on September 11, 2001, shocked America to its core and ushered in a decade, and counting, of enormously expensive foreign wars, frayed relations between Western allies and a growing sense that religious extremism represented a limit on the progression of the capitalist ideal proposed by Fukuyama.

With the U.S. and a handful of Western allies spending trillions of dollars on military operations in Iraq and Afghanistan, President George W. Bush pursued policies designed to encourage home ownership and consumer spending as a means of buttressing the U.S. economy against the ruinous cost of these wars. Those measures—combined with the deregulation of the financial markets, high-speed electronic networks and the emergence of unregulated markets for exotic derivatives—eventually produced a credit-driven housing bubble that popped spectacularly in September 2008. The ensuing collapse triggered the worst recession since the Great Depression of the 1930s. It also gutted seemingly stable banks on both sides of the Atlantic, stripped millions of people of their savings and left huge tracts of suburban homes, a quarter of which were worth less than the value of their mortgage debt, all but deserted in the ensuing real estate collapse.

While Barack Obama, upon taking office, moved swiftly to approve unprecedented stimulus packages meant to prevent the collapse of some big banks and the U.S. car industry, Fukuyama's grand historical narrative continued to be heavily battered by events. Globalization had produced astonishingly large, and inherently destabilizing, trade imbalances, as the U.S., the world's preeminent consumer market, had all but stopped manufacturing goods in its quest for affordable leisure.

In Russia, meanwhile, the transition from a command-and-control economy to a free market had produced first a class of corrupt oligarchs and then, in Putin's permanent presidency, a profoundly

antidemocratic kleptocracy. Finally, the promise of the Internet—
frictionless markets, the radical democratization of new forms of
creativity and universal access to information once available only to
the world's elites—had generated all manner of unintended side effects: the evisceration of news organizations, the use of new social
media platforms for antisocial purposes such as cyber-bullying and
the extraordinary amplification of the sort of hate speech whose cir-
culation was once circumscribed by the cost of printing pamphlets.

Surveying the state of the world in the 2010s, a pair of promi-
nent intellectuals—the *New York Times*'s Thomas Friedman and
the geographer Richard Florida—saw radically different land-
scapes: Friedman described a "flat" world where economic opportunity and wealth could pop up anywhere there were creative
and entrepreneurial people. Florida, by contrast, saw a "spiky"
world where wealth and opportunity pooled, producing zones
of immense privilege and other areas of grinding deprivation. In
Florida's darker view, globalization wasn't evenly distributing the
fruits of galloping productivity and technological advancement;
rather, those who knew how to benefit succeeded in persuading
politicians to double down on the policies that had produced the
form of global trade that exists today.

By now, it's fairly evident that big rewards are flowing to a
global class of professionals with lots of education, adaptable skills
and knowledge, the capacity for risk taking and access to capital.
It's also clear that, in many cases, a certain amount of earned privilege flows from inherited privilege: to earn that sterling transcript
from Harvard, it helps to have gone to the right preschool. And as
Thomas Piketty has pointed out, even as the stars of the knowledge economy pull away from their fellow workers, accumulated

wealth is pulling away from *all* workers as returns to invested capital increasingly outpace returns to labour. In short, globalization
has created both losers and winners, and the former are variously
looking for scapegoats or leaders who can articulate and champion
their disenfranchisement.

As the first decade of the twenty-first century drew to a close,
history didn't seem to be unspooling its concluding acts. In 2011,
about a generation after Fukuyama's book, a Tunisian street
vendor ignited the so-called Arab Spring. In rapid succession, a
populist and digitally savvy revolution moved from one Middle
Eastern or North African nation to another. But, as had been
the case in Iran during the so-called Green Movement of 2009,
the early optimism of peaceful crowds quickly produced state repression, sectarian violence and, in the case of Libya, the fall of
a dictator and a volatile power vacuum. The Arab Spring's nadir,
of course, occurred in Syria, where the nascent antiregime opposition spawned brutal new repression and a chaotic civil war. All
the while, ISIS, a new and shockingly sadistic form of terrorist
insurgency, dug itself into parts of Syria, Iraq and even Turkey,
carrying out a program of mass executions and kidnappings in
an effort to create a caliphate.

ISIS exported violence, imported newly radicalized jihadists
recruited from the Middle East, Europe and even here in North
America, and forced an exodus of refugees not seen since World
War II. All those people floated, swam and walked through mis-
erable conditions towards the promise of safety in Western nations that, in many cases, were not especially keen to accept them.
So, twenty-five years after George H. W. Bush pledged a "peace
dividend" in the wake of communism's collapse, the world now

seems more like a place with little peace and dividends that accrue mainly to those with the means to protect their earned and inherited privileges.

UNLIKE THE OPTIMISTIC revolt that toppled the rotting institutions of communism in the late 1980s, the populism of the mid-2010s is marked by fear, economic uncertainty and shopping lists of resentments directed at others (immigrants, refugees, visible minorities, Muslims, Roma, LGBTQ+ people, etc.). Social values research also shows that this wave is driven by a desire for authoritarian leaders in a world that has become too fast paced and jumbled for many people, especially those who see diversity and a global outlook as a personal threat.

In the U.K., for example, concern about immigration barely registered in the early 1990s—only 4 per cent said it was the most important issue facing the country—when the members of the European Union signed the Maastricht Treaty that would eventually lead to monetary union and the opening of cross-border labour markets. But Brits became increasingly anxious about immigration throughout the 2000s, and the number saying immigration had become the most important issue exceeded 40 per cent by 2008.[2] While the severe post-2008 recession forced residents of the British Isles to focus on the economy, by 2016 concern over immigration again topped the list—hardly surprising, given the outcome of the Brexit referendum.

According to Oxford University's Migration Observatory, Britain's population includes a segment with long-standing negative attitudes about newcomers, but those feelings have risen sharply in recent years, with one 2013 survey showing that 77 per cent wanted immigration reduced by either a lot or a little. About the same number feared illegal immigration, and only 4.1 per cent wanted increased immigration. Those negative attitudes—the highest in Europe—contrast sharply to Canada, where, in 2017, 62 per cent disagreed with the statement that immigration levels are too high, 78 per cent believed newcomers have a positive economic impact and fear of illegitimate refugee claimants has been *dropping* sharply for most of this decade.

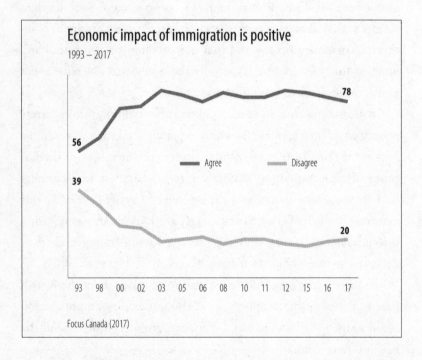

Economic impact of immigration is positive
1993 – 2017

Focus Canada (2017)

The Brexit referendum—a cynical political ploy by former prime minister David Cameron that backfired spectacularly—was ostensibly about Britain's membership in a remote and top-heavy bureaucratic institution, one that the Leave side alleged was draining resources from the U.K. treasury and harming services like health care.

In the aftermath, it became clear that pollsters and journalists had misread public and elite opinion, failing to understand how older, white, rural voters had come to resent the world of younger, multi-ethnic urbanites. In the long tradition of British rabble-rousers, UKIP leader Nigel Farage gave voice to all those xenophobic fears and sublimated them into an attack on the EU and all the apparent problems it exported across the English Channel, including a stream of job- and service-seeking immigrants from Eastern Europe, Africa and the Middle East.

Theresa May emerged from the postreferendum chaos as Conservative leader and prime minister. As she embarked on the long slog of withdrawing from the EU and renegotiating the U.K.'s complex web of relationships with Brussels, that separatist, xenophobic fervor seemed to yield to something that looked like a bit of a political hangover. May sought a new mandate in a May 2017 general election to shore up her political authority as her government proceeded to negotiate its divorce from the Continent. But in the wake of two terrorist attacks during a terrible campaign, May had to scramble to explain deep cuts she had authorized to police budgets; she emerged with a minority government and an emboldened Labour Party led by Jeremy Corbyn.

In Continental Europe, public concern about immigrants, which simmers on the back burner in many nations, reached a boiling point in recent years due to a combination of factors including long-standing cultural animosities and the surge of refugees seeking safe havens. This most recent rightwards shift, however, is part of a longer-term phenomenon, as populist right political parties across Europe have seen steady gains in their share of votes cast since the 1970s. In fact, public support for those parties consistently exceeds electoral backing for left-wing populist parties.[3]

That drift has been especially evident in places like Hungary, a country with a long tradition of institutionalized and cultural bigotry. The post-Communist era, marred by a chronically stalled economy and political scandals, has seen a growing number of attacks on minorities (Roma, Jews) and the rise of ultraconservative authoritarian rule under Viktor Orbán and Fidesz, the party he formed in the early 1990s to promote economic liberalization. When the stream of Syrian and North African refugees swelled into a torrent in 2015, authorities were quick to respond with aggressive measures to block and harass migrants, a stance that was popular with many Hungarians.

Poland has also seen a rise in anti-elitist/conspiracy-minded politics since a plane crash in 2010 took the life of President Lech Kaczyński, leaving a power vacuum that has since been filled by his twin brother, Jaroslaw Kaczyński, a member of an opposition party. Kaczyński, as head of the nationalist Law and Justice Party, has targeted outsiders, elites and the members of the tiny remaining Jewish community as his parliamentary lieutenants have moved to consolidate power and whip up anti-immigrant, anti-EU sentiment. Poland, considered for many years to be one of the most successful post-Soviet Eastern European nations with "relatively positive" attitudes towards immigrants,[4] has pursued authoritarian policies and rolled back democratic freedoms, with Law and Justice pursuing a campaign of harassment against the former pro-EU government.

"In its revolt against European liberalism, the party stands at the forefront of a growing movement," the *New York Times*'s James Traub observed of Law and Justice. "The one unifying feature of Western democracies today is the rise of nativist, nationalist parties. All of them tap a deep and thickening vein of pessimism about the economic and political prospects of the West." Traub identifies the "aftershocks" of the credit crisis and the "fierce back-lash" against refugees and newcomers. "[Such] anxieties about a globalized world have created a bull market in nostalgia."[5]

Turkey, like Poland situated between the East and West, has also experienced this kind of democratic backsliding in the wake of an accelerating political crisis. Mass demonstrations in Istanbul's Taksim Square in 2013 were met with increased repression and finally a push by the country's long-standing leader, Recep Tayyip Erdoğan, to seek approval to significantly expand the powers of the president. In a country struggling to accommodate millions of Syrian refugees and suffering repeated incursions by ISIS forces, the narrow victory—Erdoğan's camp won 51.4 per cent of the votes—transformed Turkey from a democracy into a much more authoritarian state. Not long after his referendum victory, Turkey blocked Wikipedia because the government disapproved of content in the entry about the country.[6]

Victories such as Erdoğan's provide more evidence that a number of states with either established, fledgling or flawed democracies are slipping towards authoritarian or despotic rule. The tenuous democracy of Boris Yeltsin's Russia was demolished by Putin, a classic strongman who has suppressed dissent, ordered the arrest and murder of journalists and reasserted quasi-dictatorial control over the national government. In the Philippines, a democracy since decades of military dictatorship came to an end in 1986, President Roberto Duterte won power in 2016, vowing to battle narcotics and violent crime. But he's fulfilled that promise by declaring open season on anyone involved in drugs, unleashing vigilantes and death squads that have summarily murdered thousands of people in a shockingly bloody "extrajudicial" campaign of terror. Meanwhile, in Chechnya, which has never been a democracy, President Ramzan Kadyrov succeeded in upping the ante on despotic conduct by herding gay men into concentration camps, where many have been killed.

These are not disparate phenomena. In many parts of the developed world, ultranationalist populist sentiment has been on the rise, accompanied by a fracturing of centrist consensus and the growth of both radical left- and right-wing populist movements. An extensive 2015 survey of fifty-six thousand people in twenty-four countries on both sides of the Atlantic noted a series of trends in public opinion that cut across national borders: political paralysis due to a new divide between "patriots" and "egalitarians"; loss of faith in traditional Western elites; a worldwide backlash against globalization; the profound impact of digital disruption (e.g., Wikileaks, fake news sites, social media algorithms that sort news according to user preferences) on traditional political and electoral systems; and the inability of mainstream political parties to address these new realities.[7]

In Europe—with its open borders, fluid labour markets and influx of both economic migrants and refugees—immigration has played a large role in driving these political responses. Non-EU citizens account for about 4 per cent of the EU's combined population. Thirty-seven per cent of working-age non-EU citizens aren't well educated. Not surprisingly, among these populations, poverty and social exclusion are high and participation in the workforce is low.[8]

The Migrant Policy Index (MIPEX) was established in 2004 by a coalition of British and European academics and NGOs to track immigration policies in the EU and selected other developed nations. Its most recent report observes that far-right parties have "never done better" in contemporary EU history, positioning themselves as "kingmakers" in a succession of national and regional elections. But analysis by MIPEX and the European Social Survey also shows that in many EU countries, public opinion about immigration also tends to be "uninformed," with many respondents to surveys overestimating the number of newcomers, the perceived criminality associated with immigrants and the cost of services such as housing and welfare directed to such individuals.

Not surprisingly, traditional immigrant-receiving nations (Canada, the U.S., Australia), as well as the Scandinavian countries, score higher on MIPEX's annual rankings of welcoming integration policies than ethnically homogenous countries that have only recently become destinations for migrants (Canada ranked sixth of thirty-eight in 2014).[9] But, as MIPEX notes, "Political will may matter more than a country's tradition of immigration, since more inclusive integration policies may encourage more immigrants to settle permanently and the public to trust immigrants more."

That finding is key, because it underscores the reality that politicians and governments can choose to push back against anti-immigrant populist backlash or they can pander to it, with increasingly predictable results. It's a choice between greater inequality and more fear on the one hand or increased social cohesion and economic mobility on the other. Perhaps not coincidentally, nativist parties have tended to be more successful in EU countries that aren't near the top of the MIPEX rankings.

In Denmark, which ranks below other Scandinavian nations and Germany on the MIPEX, the anti-immigrant far-right Danish People's Party made huge gains in the 2015 general elections, increasing its share of the popular vote from 12.3 per cent (2011) to 21.2 per cent and positioning itself as the second-largest party in Parliament—its best result by far since its founding in the 1990s.

The Netherlands' Party for Freedom, led by Geert Wilders, made similarly impressive inroads in the spring 2017 election, emerging as the second-place party with 13 per cent of the popular vote and 20 of the 150 seats in the national legislature. While some polls predicted that Wilders might even win, Mark Rutte, who leads the front-running conservative party, tacked hard right late in the race and secured a victory by pandering to anti-immigrant sentiment. The backdrop is not incidental: according to MIPEX, the Netherlands in the early 2010s abandoned its long-standing commitment to highly progressive immigrant integration policies.

Meanwhile, in Austria, a far-right party led by Norbert Hofer placed first in the opening round of voting in the January 2016 general election. The result was praised by nationalist and far-right politicians across Europe, including France's Marine Le Pen. Hofer lost in the second round after voters coalesced around the Greens, but it's significant that Hofer won 46 per cent of the popular vote. Again, these results are rooted in earlier shifts in values. According to the 2014 version of the European Social Survey, Austria was one of a handful of EU nations where the proportion of people who felt immigrants made the country worse had increased between 2002 and 2014.

Certainly the most watched election in Europe in the post-Brexit period was in France. The first round, held in April 2017, produced a historic outcome for Le Pen's National Front. In the seven years since she ousted her father (also the party's founder), Le Pen has sought to recast the party as less explicitly racist, even as details of the party's anti-Semitism continue to surface. Targeting younger disillusioned voters as well as the National Front's traditional base (rural, southern and older voters), Le Pen came away with 21.3 per cent of the votes cast, an all-time high for the forty-four-year-old party and enough to win a berth in the run-off against Emmanuel Macron, a thirty-nine-year-old investment banker who ran as an outspoken proponent of the EU. Though he won the run-off with two-thirds of the votes cast (and this despite a mysterious last-minute release of unflattering emails from his campaign), Macron's victory fell short of previous outcomes, when voters opposed to the National Front rallied around the mainstream candidate in a gesture of solidarity. Despite those results, Macron moved quickly to establish himself on the global stage, drawing the kind of star-struck attention that greeted Justin Trudeau after his 2015 victory. For his efforts, Macron's party, En Marche, secured a strong centrist victory in France's June 2017, parliamentary elections. (Parties on both the far left and far right also saw gains.)

In contrast to the Brexit referendum or the 2016 American presidential race, public opinion polls in France predicted Le Pen's rise with a fair degree of precision, including a bump in the closing days. The problems with public opinion polling in the age of cell phones and digital media are well known, but the accuracy of the French polling suggests that Le Pen supporters didn't feel the need to be cagey about their preferences.

In the U.S., polling companies, as well as media prognosticators who had developed complex predictive models, severely misjudged both the depth of Trump's support and the tenuousness of Clinton's. With mainstream media outlets almost unanimous in their condemnation of Trump, polling firms also were hampered in making accurate forecasts because many voters who quietly backed him weren't saying so. The national numbers, which correctly showed Clinton ahead in the popular vote (she won by nearly three million votes), did not reveal the all-important horse races in Pennsylvania, Michigan and Wisconsin. In the U.K., pollsters and pundits also misjudged the dynamics of the Brexit referendum, dismissing the likelihood of a Leave victory.

In both cases, the polling and analytics may have fed into a self-reinforcing dynamic: with much analysis in the information environment downplaying the likelihood of either a Trump or Brexit victory, supporters for Clinton and the Remain forces may have been lulled into a sense of complacency. Turnout in many traditional Democratic strongholds was low, with many young Bernie Sanders supporters failing to back Clinton. In the immediate aftermath of the U.K. referendum, news organizations found many examples of voters who regretted casting ballots for Leave; they'd done so only to send a signal to the British political elites, not because they actually wanted to leave the EU. For both votes, public opinion was almost evenly divided and thus vulnerable to imponderables, such as the proliferation of fake news sites and Russian incursions or the hacking of the Democratic Party's emails.

The story in France was somewhat different. As *Globe and Mail* foreign affairs columnist Doug Saunders pointed out, the geographical distribution of anti-immigrant/xenophobic voters has remained remarkably fixed for more than a century. Regional voting patterns can be traced back to the Dreyfus Affair in the 1890s, through the support for Vichy in World War II, and on to the modern-day National Front's core constituencies in the northeast and south of France.[10] Meanwhile, French perceptions about immigrants from poorer countries vary dramatically between older, less well-educated residents and younger, more educated ones. In fact, aside from Slovenia, the gap is larger in France than all the other EU nations that participated in the European Social Survey. A large gap indicates a lack of consensus about policies—countries like Hungary and Lithuania have a very small gap because most people oppose immigration, regardless of their demographic.[11]

But there's more to growing French nativism than merely these factors. France's non-EU migrant population tends to be less well educated (and thus more economically and socially marginalized), which is a reflection of the country's geographical location, as well as migration patterns connected to its colonial past.

More than most EU nations, France restricts and delays labour market integration for non-EU immigrants, limits their access to education and throws up roadblocks to family re-unification. "These delays," concluded MIPEX, "put newcomers on an unequal footing, with potentially negative long-term effects."[12] In other words, public policy choices have reinforced these divides, thus creating a vicious cycle. But the opposite dynamic is also possible—more enlightened immigrant settlement policies can produce improved living standards, which translate into greater acceptance and integration, and thus support for more progressive policies.

Beyond the particular impact of public policy on immigrant integration, some analysts point out that in many European countries, the fundamental notion of multiculturalism (a term whose definition is capacious and ambiguous, and varies from place to place) remains controversial and unpopular—a pejorative label for a social experiment that has failed despite countless official EU policy declarations.

Queen's University psychologist John Berry points out that multiculturalism can succeed only in societies that go beyond tolerating newcomers and actually find ways to encourage meaningful two-way engagement between immigrants and the dominant group(s). Newcomers tend to be more successful when they seek to connect with mainstream society instead of remaining at a remove from it. When there's more positive contact between newcomer groups and the mainstream, prejudices and hostility begin to fall away and a sense of belonging grows. Conversely, in societies where newcomers or minorities remain segregated—in social housing complexes, low-wage work or ghettos—any contact that does occur is likely to be fraught with suspicion and fear.[13] As Berry concludes, if societies forge public policies grounded in the underlying psychology of intercultural engagement, they'll have a better chance of becoming genuinely multicultural. If the multicultural project does not run deeper than words in high-level documents or national charters, there's a much greater likelihood of failure and therefore political backlash.

OUR RESEARCH REVEALS considerable similarity in social values and outlooks in Americans inclined to support Donald Trump and Europeans drawn to far-right parties. Both groups tend to express a high level of national pride, a desire for strong leadership and a disdain for the intelligentsia and elites, who, they say, are blinded by their own political correctness. They espouse traditional values, have concerns about immigration and mistrust government. These voters disagree with the idea that every person in the world deserves equal treatment, and they resolutely do not see themselves as cosmopolitan—they are citizens not of the world but of the country in which they live. Interestingly, the economy doesn't necessarily register as a significant concern for either far-right Europeans or Trump supporters—an indication that political rhetoric about the loss of manufacturing jobs due to outsourcing or trade deals is serving as a convenient xenophobic code to mobilize voters who feel a loss of status in a globalized world.

At face value, those similarities seem to confirm the notion that we're watching a large and transnational phenomenon—a highly infectious backlash against globalization, mass migration and terrorism. After all, the contrasts between the U.S. and most EU nations could scarcely be greater. The U.S. is, theoretically, a melting pot nation of immigrants that carries the residual pain of slavery, a dedication to free markets and individualism and a hostility towards centralized government regulation. While some EU countries have colonial legacies that have influenced immigration patterns for years, most still retain a strong sense of ethnocultural and linguistic identity, support a centralized, activist government and have participated in post–World War II multilateral institutions for nearly three-quarters of a century. Where American values run in the direction of the Second Amendment (the right to bear arms), Protestant fundamentalism and the open road to frontiers of freedom, Europeans are more likely to fret about climate change and defend their state-sponsored pensions and other perks.

So the story of how Americans chose Donald Trump to succeed the first black president—and did so despite the fact that Barack Obama's approval rating by the end of his term was almost 56 per cent[14]—bears unpacking. After all, if the U.S. can shift gears so radically, Canada must be vulnerable, too. Or is it? We need to know exactly how the backlash unfolded in the U.S. in order to determine whether Canada has similar symptoms and conditions that might put it at risk.

The first point is that Trumpism, despite all the red meat rhetoric about bringing back American manufacturing jobs with tough new trade terms, was never actually about economic angst.

Indeed, a growing body of evidence now shows that racial intolerance, not the labour markets or income inequality, was a key driving factor in the backlash behind the 2016 election, as well as many of the recent races in Europe. The renowned social values researcher Ronald Inglehart has found that the Trump/Brexit era reflects a widespread and potent "cultural backlash"—especially prevalent among older, white, lower-educated males—to the postmaterialism of recent decades, and especially heightened political attention to noneconomic issues, such as multiculturalism, LGBTQ+ rights, climate change and, most obviously, feminism.

Confronted with a technologically turbo-charged world, dramatically divergent media representations of current affairs and seemingly uncontrollable challenges to traditional ways of life, many people choose to express their unease by supporting political movements and leaders who promise a return of the "good old days," even if those days were little more than airbrushed mythologies.

This kind of backlash happened previously in postwar America. In the early 1970s, Richard Nixon waged a culture war against cosmopolitan elites in the name of the "silent majority." A decade later, Ronald Reagan—a more convincing and sunnier populist than Nixon—made speeches invoking "morning in America," even as his operatives succeeded in converting millions of working-class, southern, white Democrats with unsubtle appeals to lingering racial prejudices ("welfare queens").

Nixon and Reagan both came to power in periods of deep economic uncertainty, eras marked by gas shortages and stagflation. In 2016, exit polls and various postelection analyses confirmed that Trump owed his victory more to white resentment and cultural apprehensions about things such as gay marriage and trans rights than to the much-hyped economic dislocation of American workers. The U.S. economy circa 2016 was firing on all cylinders, with low unemployment, high job creation, modest interest rates and a resurgence of the housing market, which had been laid to waste after the 2008 credit crisis.

It's crucial to remember that Trump first came into political focus with the 2012 birther movement, a force on the right that he did so much to engineer, and then via his explicit appeals to racist and Islamophobic impulses after declaring his candidacy. The birthers drew their energy from the Tea Party movement, which was also redolent of appeals to racism and nostalgia for a segregated past. Trump began his nomination campaign by accusing Mexico of exporting murderers and rapists to the U.S., and even since taking office, his anti-immigrant, anti-Muslim rhetoric hasn't subsided.

Education levels also played a crucial role in fueling Trump's brand of xenophobic populism. Those without college degrees—the single strongest indicator of a Trump supporter, as *The Atlantic* observed during the primaries[15]—are much more likely to support authoritarian leadership styles and a strong leader who doesn't have to worry about negotiating with Congress or even allow elections. The presence of these attitudes in Trump's base helps to explain why he hasn't balked at making overtures to strongmen like the Philippines' Duterte and even North Korea's Kim Jong-un.

More generally, Trumpism has found fertile ground in the vast and widening social divides in American society: rural vs. urban, white vs. multi-ethnic, educated vs. uneducated, gun owners vs. gun control advocates, pro-life vs. pro-choice, Fox/Breitbart viewers vs. MSNBC/*New York Times* subscribers, red states vs. blue states. Most democracies toggle between parties on the left and right, which is healthy and normal. But when there's so little space left in the centre, the winners inevitably reflect, amplify and re-inforce all that polarization, even though large numbers of voters may also see this kind of fracturing as a troubling development.[16]

These splits are increasingly baked into every aspect of American civic life. Consider Americans' increasingly conflicted notions of national identity. According to recent surveys, space for consensus has become increasingly difficult to locate. Even bedrock values such as freedom of expression have come under attack from both right and left.[17]

These fissures have been evident for decades. Republicans, and Trump supporters in particular, have long expressed xenophobic impulses as well as a strong preference for traditional families, obedience to authority, patriotism and cultural assimilation. Hillary Clinton's backers were much more inclined to espouse postmaterialist values, such as multiculturalism and ecological awareness.

The backlash that produced Trump was apparent in the pronounced reversal in attitudes on a range of social values that occurred from 2004 to 2012. This period, bifurcated by the great recession, was marked by a sharp drop in the acceptance of violence and the valuing of ostentatious consumption, as well as a moderate decline in xenophobia, sexism and patriarchy. In the same period, Americans grew more likely to embrace forms of personal expression and ecological concern, and, overall, a surprising shift towards self-fulfillment.

From 2012 to 2016, however, the forces that produced both Trump and Vermont senator Bernie Sanders were percolating. On one side of the great divide, we saw a general decline in traditional values and more support for flexible, nontraditional families and sexual permissiveness—evidence of the increasing influence of the millennials. Greater financial security, an increase in risk taking and consumption also emerged as the 2009 recession ebbed. But at the same time, more Americans were expressing patriarchal, bigoted and parochial outlooks, despite a steadily improving economy. By 2016, fifty per cent of Americans agreed the father must be the master in his own house—a strong indicator of support for populist authoritarian politicians who are unafraid to whip up anti-feminist, anti-immigrant/nationalist sentiment.

THESE ARE THE values that put Trump into office, gave the Leave side its Brexit victory and contributed to the steady increase in the electoral support of once marginal nationalist and anti-immigrant parties in some, though not all, EU countries.

The question is whether these diffuse forces have peaked or if the appeal of this cast of politics will continue to spread. Will the National Front and the likes of Norbert Hofer or Geert Wilders make even more gains in the elections in the early 2020s? Will Donald Trump—an erratic demagogue who doesn't hide his admiration of dictators because he knows many of his followers share his views—move to consolidate executive power and push the U.S. government towards autocracy? Or will the political pendulum swing back to something more centrist and normalized?

The new populism draws its momentum from free-floating anxieties about modernity and global change that don't stop at national borders. Yet it's equally clear that state-level governments and societies aren't mere flotsam bobbing haplessly in the path of a violent storm. Countries have choices. During the 1988 federal election, liberal leader John Turner told Canadians that free trade with the United States would obliterate the Canada-U.S. border and threaten our cherished national institutions, most notably our beloved national health-care system known as Medicare. The plurality of Canadians didn't believe him and backed Brian Mulroney, effectively voting for free trade. In the ensuing decades, Canada has continued to go its own way on a wide range of social and economic policies, and our commitment to Medicare is as strong as ever. For Canadians, it seems that being more connected—and being subject to certain transnational pressures, ideas and debates—doesn't mean losing all autonomy.

Most EU countries face some measure of pressure from transnational forces like mass migration. Some have opted to implement and defend policies that foster integration and acceptance while others have reverted to measures that encourage fear, exclusion and harassment. Either choice creates a cascading cycle that becomes self-reinforcing and self-perpetuating.

None of this is to discount the historically or geographically specific narratives of individual nations: the legacies of French colonialism or American slavery, for example, continue to influence both countries' political dynamics, cultural expression and social values. Similarly, nations whose borders aren't under constant pressure—and Canada certainly falls into this category—may fret less about migrants, not because of some kind of moral superiority but rather due to an accident of geography.

But the story doesn't end with history or geography, neither of which is destiny. It *is* possible for nations to undergo significant social change and yet emerge more cohesive, buttressed by robust democracies that are capable of power sharing even as they withstand the hate-filled, fragmenting politics of exclusion.

Canada's experience, in the three decades since NAFTA, reveals such a narrative, one that shows how a country can—with a mix of foresight, pragmatic compromise and, frankly, good luck—endure a brush with disintegration, populist-inflected national politics, dramatic social change due to immigration and the economic uncertainties associated with open borders. Any one of these elements alone could have provoked retrenchment, fear and backlash. And yet it didn't happen, which is why Canada's story, at this fraught moment, is so worth telling.

CHAPTER TWO

We've Been Here Before

It was, quite possibly, one of the nerdiest controversies ever to hit the front pages of Canadian newspapers.

In June 2010, the Harper government announced, via an order-in-council, that Canadians would no longer be required to complete the so-called long-form census. These detailed household questionnaires are distributed every five years. They form the backbone of Statistics Canada's detailed census documents, which government officials, businesses and social service agencies use to gauge everything from where to place tuberculosis clinics to where the need for affordable housing is most urgent to where to open a new Starbucks. For as long as anyone could remember, the long-form census not only existed, but was compulsory—you had to fill it out. In its place, the Conservatives said StatsCan would use a simplified and optional "national household survey."

Industry Minister Tony Clement, a senior member of the Conservative cabinet, sought to spin the decision as a response to concerns from individuals about the statutory penalties for not completing the census. "There have been more and more complaints each round [of the census] every five years," he said. "We have had many, many complaints about the census but I can't quantify the exact number."[1]

But his critics—everyone from editorial writers to municipal planners, marketers and opposition politicians—weren't buying that line and fulminated against the Tories' decision to water down something as basic as the census. After all, as many veteran number crunchers said at the time, if policy makers didn't have a solid, statistical picture of Canada's population, they wouldn't be able to fashion and properly focus public services. StatsCan's chief statistician quit in protest.

At a time when there's substantial evidence that "fake news," some of it created by Russian operatives, has played a worrisome role in altering not just public opinion but also political decision making and even an election outcome, the long-form census controversy seems like a quaint artifact from a distant era.

But at the core of that dust-up sits a question that has become highly relevant at a time when many people live in their own information bubbles, consuming news and opinion that confirm their own views. Are we able to agree, more or less, on a common set of facts, which in turn form the basis of vigorous debates about issues such as income inequality, social services, global warming and the like?

The Harper Tories regularly made it clear that evidence-based, information-driven decision making was no longer prized. *Maclean's* called it Ottawa's "war on data."[2] Government scientists, especially those working in fields related to climate science, were forbidden from publicly discussing their findings, an edict that brought condemnation from Canadian and international researchers. Some repositories of scientific data and reports were pulped in the name of cost cutting.

The Conservatives also passed almost a hundred tough-on-crime laws designed to telegraph the message that Canadian courts will have to enforce mandatory minimums and cease the practice of approving time-served reductions for sentences for violent offenders. When the opposition parties and criminologists noted that violent crime had reached historic lows and pointed to U.S. evidence showing the negative consequences of harsh sentencing, the government doubled down. These new laws, Conservative officials said, were necessary to address the *perception* of rising crime and also to serve as a potent deterrent. Both arguments, however, lacked a compelling factual basis.[3]

As the government shifted from grounding its public policy choices in evidence, and then went so far as to interfere with the gathering of said evidence, many Canadians balked. After the decision to cancel the long-form census, public opinion polls showed that almost six in ten Canadians disapproved. And contrary to government claims, only a quarter regarded a mandatory census as intrusive.[4] Public support for reinstating the census remained high enough that both opposition parties made it a cornerstone of their re-election platforms in 2015.

Restoring the long-form census was, in fact, one of the new Liberal government's first acts in office. Not only did the opposition Conservatives not oppose the decision, former Harper ministers, including Clement, went public with their discomfort at the original move and expressed regret for supporting it. "I think I would have done it differently, looking back on it," Clement told the *Huffington Post*.[5]

SUCH EPISODES OFFER clues about the outer limits of conservative Canadian populism and how far this agenda can extend before hitting an electoral nerve.

To a great extent, contemporary Canadian populism traces back to the late 1980s, when Preston Manning—the cerebral son of Alberta's longtime Social Credit premier Ernest Manning—founded the Reform Party, a western populist movement. The Reform's predominantly white members opposed special status for Quebec, official multiculturalism, centralized government and Brian Mulroney's Progressive Conservatives. Some individual members expressed hostility towards non-European immigrants and espoused socially conservative views. Manning and top party officials adamantly denied that the party was intolerant and generally steered clear of anything that smelled like a moral agenda.

Reform's popularity spread to Ontario, where Mike Harris's Tories, in the mid-1990s, succeeded in tapping into the party's forceful appeal to fiscal conservatives who mistrusted big government. After years of attempts by conservative activists, including Harper (a former Manning aide), to mend the split on the right—the Canadian Alliance (successor to Reform) merged with the Progressive Conservatives and later re-emerged as the Conservative Party under Harper's leadership.

While conservative Americans have split dramatically in recent years, especially after the emergence of the Tea Party in 2010, the move on Canada's right to smooth over internal ideological divisions has prevented the kind of sectarian rupture that has taken place in the Republican Party.

Abortion is a case in point. In the U.S., abortion remains one of the most politically radioactive issues in that country's public life, even four decades after the landmark *Roe v. Wade* Supreme Court ruling. As of 2016, only 41 per cent of Americans supported a woman's right to choose. During the GOP primaries, Donald

Trump mused in a TV interview that women should be punished for obtaining an abortion (he later retracted the statement).[6] In office, however, one of his first executive orders halted aid to international agencies that provide or "promote" abortions; he and congressional Republicans have also threatened to de-fund Planned Parenthood.

The trajectory of abortion rights in Canada could scarcely be more different. After years of legal challenges brought by the reproductive rights advocate Henry Morgentaler, the Supreme Court struck down Canada's abortion laws in 1988. The Mulroney government reintroduced legislation but it failed to pass in the Senate and no government since has touched the matter, despite the fact that social conservatives continue to be well represented among the constituents of Conservative MPs in ridings in southern Alberta and southwestern Ontario.

Despite that, 57 per cent of Canadians support abortion rights "under any circumstances" and that figure has risen steadily in recent years.[7] Not coincidentally, gender equality is our most important aspirational value, with 92 per cent of respondents strongly supportive of the idea that Canada should be a country in which men and women are treated equally in all walks of life. It's hardly a surprise that a society that highly values one of sort of equity—gender—is also positively predisposed towards recognizing that people from diverse ethnocultural or immigrant backgrounds also deserve acceptance from the social mainstream.

There's a similar narrative with the death penalty, which was last imposed in the early 1960s. In 1976, Parliament decided in a free vote to abolish the death penalty: 131 in favour to 124 opposed. Liberals and Progressive Conservatives fell on both sides of the issue, while New Democrats were solidly in favour of abolition.

Public opinion was elsewhere entirely. In 1979, seventy-seven per cent of Canadians were in favour of capital punishment for certain crimes, while only 19 per cent were opposed.

Not all Canadians were altogether enamoured of these approaches. Still, they deferred to a loose coalition of the educated, the urban, and Quebec progressives, who were heavily represented in legislatures, government bureaucracies and the courts. Those elites, in turn, deferred to evidence, including those darn statistics so beloved by criminologists (a collective response that perhaps anticipated public outrage over the long-form census). Over time, Canadians have generally warmed to the progressive policies of the last several decades, even if they were opposed to or divided about them when they were first introduced.

That consensus, observed University of Toronto criminologist Anthony Doob in *Policy Options*, recognized that (i) social conditions, and not just individual choices, impact crime; (ii) harsh punishments don't serve as a useful deterrent; and (iii) the "development of criminal justice policies should be informed by expert knowledge."

Successive governments, both Liberal and Tory, opted not to reintroduce the death penalty—evidence of a long-standing agreement about advancing a progressive criminal justice system that's based on expert analyses and statistical data, not the whims of angry voters. While Harper said he personally favoured the death penalty in some cases, he didn't re-open the debate in Parliament. Since the mid-1970s, support for the death penalty has dropped twenty-four points. While a slim majority still supports the death penalty "for certain crimes," Canadians are not clamoring for capital punishment for murderers in general. When asked in 2007, a year after Harper's first minority victory, to name the most appropriate punishment for a convicted murderer, 69 per cent of Canadians chose "life imprisonment with no possibility of parole," while 24 per cent chose the death penalty. In 2010, just over half of Canadians (53 per cent) favoured the death penalty for certain crimes. Harper realized that the death penalty, which has been abandoned in many U.S. states because of botched lethal injection executions, was a non-starter in his home and native land.

However, the Harper Conservatives sought to capitalize at the polls by nurturing populist resentments and doling out politically incorrect red meat to reap the political rewards. His party was more than willing to dismiss educated urban elites who had had the ear of government for decades. Harper's gambit was to activate that segment of his base that prefers its policy to reflect "common sense" instead of crime trend data and the progressive prescriptions of ivory-tower crime experts. "We're not governing on the basis of the latest statistics," Justice Minister Rob Nicholson said of the Tories' policies. "We're governing on the basis of what's right to better protect victims and law-abiding Canadians."

The Prime Minister let it be known that he did not need a literature review to tell him how to punish a bad guy. In place of statistics, the government offered up a leader (a "strict father," in American cognitive linguist George Lakoff's formulation) who acted on principle and conviction.

Harper also knew he could make political hay by attacking the courts. In 2014, he publicly questioned Supreme Court chief justice Beverley McLachlin over the appointment of a Quebec federal court judge to the highest court. Harper wrongly insinuated that she had improperly inserted herself in the process. That response drew widespread elite condemnation from pundits, bar associations and law professors. Describing Harper's gesture as "Nixonian," *The Globe and Mail*'s former national affairs writer Jeffrey Simpson, the ultimate Ottawa insider, was withering in his condemnation: "How low can Prime Minister Stephen Harper's government go? The answer is that just when you think new depths of conduct have been plumbed, even lower ones are found."[8] Only 48 per cent of Canadians that year reported that they had confidence in the Supreme Court, up from 31 per cent in 2012 but still less than a majority.[9]

But as the Tories would discover, a government's appeal to populist, anti-elite sentiment—a stance that delivers millions of votes in the U.S., where authoritarian leadership styles have far greater appeal than in Canada—has limited reach here. Relatively early on, Harper's 2008 campaign promise to stiffen sentences for violent youth offenders aged fourteen and over played badly in Quebec, and may have even cost him seats in that province and therefore a majority in the general election. In later years, moreover, many of the Conservative party's tough-on-crime laws were overturned by the courts.

In fact, long before their appeal to anti-Muslim sentiment during the 2015 federal election, the Harper Tories were bumping up against the ongoing consolidation of generally progressive social values in Canada. Public opinion in recent decades seems to have steadily followed elite consensus, with majority support for the death penalty, for example, eroding over time while support for the decriminalization of prostitution and marijuana has grown. Although opinion is not overwhelmingly on one side in either case (and the numbers vary depending on the poll questions), over time Canadians' views on a range of criminal justice issues have moved towards the less punitive approaches adopted by Parliament.

Take sex work. In 2005, fifty-one per cent of Canadians said it should be legal, up eleven points from a decade earlier.

The matter came to a head in 2013, when the Supreme Court struck down three key provisions of the Criminal Code that govern prostitution. The case involved Terri-Jean Bedford, a dominatrix who had run an escort service and later something called the Bondage Bungalow, both of which employed security systems to ensure the safety of sex workers.[10]

A year later, the Tories introduced new prostitution legislation, which they described as aiming to protect women from exploitation and human trafficking. Critics, including Bedford, described the law as needlessly strict and out of step with the evidence on how to make sex work safer. But public opinion on prostitution hadn't shifted since 2005. An Angus Reid poll conducted after the bill was tabled showed an almost even split between Canadians who supported the new laws and those who felt that selling sex should be legal, with women strongly opposed to the legislation as drafted. Crucially, the law didn't appeal to party members. "Even among those who voted Conservative in the last election, only 45 per cent support the bill, while 37 per cent are against." The result offered further evidence that conservative populist sentiment in Canada can take you only so far.

When the Liberals took office in 2015, they announced they'd revisit the Tories' law,[11] drawing on peer-reviewed evidence about the nature of sex work produced by the Canadian Institute for Health Research,[12] a move that further reinforced the notion that Canadians and Canadian policy makers remain comfortable tethering public policy to expert opinion rather than just moral, religious or emotional arguments.

As for the decriminalization of the "personal use" of marijuana, Harper insisted such a move would not happen under his government, although the Conservatives did set up a regulatory system for the production and distribution of medical marijuana, a good deal of which is used for recreational purposes. After Trudeau—then the leader of the third party in Parliament—announced that a Liberal government would decriminalize marijuana and establish "smart" drug policies, Harper and his strategists moved quickly to paint him as naïve and soft on crime. However, with six out of ten Canadians supportive of decriminalization, Trudeau knew he had public opinion on his side.

But the Liberals' gambit on pot was grounded in something more fundamental to Canada's dominant political culture: rejection of the retributive Protestant moralism that goes all the way back to the Puritans in Salem and has long informed important aspects of American public life, including the war on drugs and a generation of three-strikes/tough-on-crime laws. It is not a coincidence that religious (Christian) observance in the U.S. remains far higher than in Canada (and in most developed nations). In fact, post–Quiet Revolution Quebec has gone so far towards banishing religion that it is the province most likely to look askance at public displays of religiosity.

Consequently, it's far more likely to hear Canadian politicians on the right describe themselves as fiscally conservative and socially progressive. There are, of course, pockets of socially conservative voters and elected officials, but not enough to use their numbers to dominate public discourse. Those federal politicians who have appealed to populist instincts either steered away from social conservatism or got burned by it when they didn't. In either case, their excesses eventually bumped up against the elitist desire to choose order and good government over more populist or republican credos.

Few illustrations of this instinct could be more telling than John Tory succeeding Rob Ford as mayor of the country's biggest city. To the surprise of many, voters took populism out for a boozy what-happens-in-Vegas-stays-in-Vegas-style long weekend. But they decided they were far more comfortable with the sort of respectability and social graces that won't rile the masses. We've been there before. And then we've come back.

CHAPTER THREE

Canada and Immigration in the Era of Trump and Brexit

If we want to ask ourselves whether "it" could happen here, a good way of considering the question is to focus on what has become the hot-potato issue of this moment: immigration.

South of the border, immigration reform has been a toxic issue for years, but there's plenty of recent evidence to suggest that the controversy has ratcheted up even more in a country that once prided itself on welcoming the tired, the poor and the hungry onto its shores. Donald Trump's campaign rhetoric about Mexicans ("rapists" who bring drugs and crime), his promises (and subsequent executive orders) to ban travel to the U.S. from Muslim-majority nations, his proposed wall along the Mexican border and his vow to increase deportations of illegal immigrants all found a large and receptive audience during and after the 2016 election.

In the United Kingdom, a potent theme of the 2015 Brexit referendum involved the question of whether access to British labour markets by European nationals and immigrants was harming the country. Across the English Channel, French, Dutch and German ultranationalists have increased their own anti-immigrant rhetoric. Far-right governments in Poland and Hungary have returned to old and chilling habits of scapegoating certain minority groups, including Roma and Jews.

While much of the world seems to be feeling cranky about cross-border flows of people, Canadians are still welcoming newcomers, mostly with open arms, and definitely with little hesitation when it comes to immigration levels. *The Economist* dubbed Canadians as "the last liberals,"[1] and there's little dispute that many important measures of national well-being show why we're still feeling tolerant. We have high life expectancies, the world's top life satisfaction scores and the highest average annual GDP increase per capita over the past decade. Canada offers some of the best maternity leaves in the world and ranks second on a global reputation index.

The numbers indeed tell the tale. "Between July 2015 and July 2016," observed University of Toronto sociologist Robert Brym, "Canada welcomed 320,932 immigrants—the largest annual number of new arrivals in the country's history, proportionately more than in any year since 1911, and proportionately 60 per cent more than the United States welcomed."

Canadians have not only bucked anti-immigrant politics (as Brym points out, there's no national anti-immigration party), but have done so with an immigration system that brings in ever more newcomers from Asia, Africa, the Middle East and Latin America. "Canada admitted 321,000 immigrants in the year to June 2016, nearly 1% of its population; typically 80% of them will eventually become citizens," *The Economist* reported. "A fifth of Canada's population is foreign-born, nearly twice the share in America." While racism and intolerance certainly do exist in Canada, including in big cities with large numbers of newcomers and visible minorities, we're nevertheless an unusual case of a colonial nation whose government and policy frameworks were shaped by people with relatively homogeneous European roots (Indigenous peoples were more diverse but politically excluded) evolving to accommodate people from incredibly diverse backgrounds, and transform all that difference into something that is generally cohesive, progressive and global.

Yet the growth of anti-immigrant sentiment elsewhere does raise urgent questions about whether these sentiments will take hold here, emboldening some Canadians to express previously suppressed or politically incorrect views.

Certainly, there have been well-documented examples of public and overt expressions of xenophobia in Canada; just consider the case of a woman who stormed into a medical clinic in Mississauga, Ont., loudly demanding a white doctor. What's more, some recent polls have showed that many Canadians aren't happy about reports of several thousand asylum seekers walking across the U.S.-Canadian border in rural Quebec and Manitoba. During the Conservative leadership campaign, some candidates sought to capitalize on this new dynamic by pledging to crack down on queue jumping and "illegal" immigration.

But are these incidents and the responses to them evidence of a real shift in social values in Canada?

The answer is no. Canadian attitudes about immigration have held steady or grown noticeably more positive after 2015, a period that saw a lot of nativist drum beating. Most Canadians continue to regard immigration as good for the economy, and there is also growing confidence in the country's ability to manage refugees and potential criminal elements.

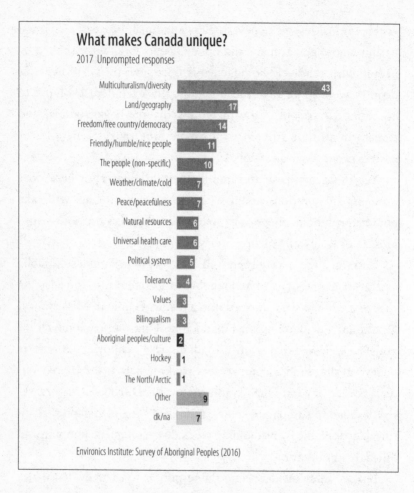

What makes Canada unique?

2017 Unprompted responses

Multiculturalism/diversity	43
Land/geography	17
Freedom/free country/democracy	14
Friendly/humble/nice people	11
The people (non-specific)	10
Weather/climate/cold	7
Peace/peacefulness	7
Natural resources	6
Universal health care	6
Political system	5
Tolerance	4
Values	3
Bilingualism	3
Aboriginal peoples/culture	2
Hockey	1
The North/Arctic	1
Other	9
dk/na	7

Environics Institute: Survey of Aboriginal Peoples (2016)

Fewer people today express concern about too many immigrants or fear that they won't adopt "Canadian values"; the
proportion articulating that opinion is now the lowest recorded
in more than twenty years. It's true that Canadians do expect
newcomers to be good citizens, which means obeying the laws,
participating actively in their communities, treating others with
respect and being tolerant of those who are different. But nine in

ten continue to say that someone born elsewhere is just as likely to be a good citizen as someone born in this country.

This outlook extends from coast to coast to coast. Residents of Atlantic Canada and British Columbia tend to be the most positive, while opinions of those in Ontario and Quebec generally fall somewhere in the middle. The three prairie provinces are at the other end of the spectrum but still tilt positive. Perspectives also vary somewhat across generations, with concerns about immigration and integration most widely voiced by older Canadians (especially those sixty-plus). But given that two in ten Canadians were born abroad (and another two in ten are their children), these expectations are often filtered through the lens of their own experiences as immigrants or second generation.

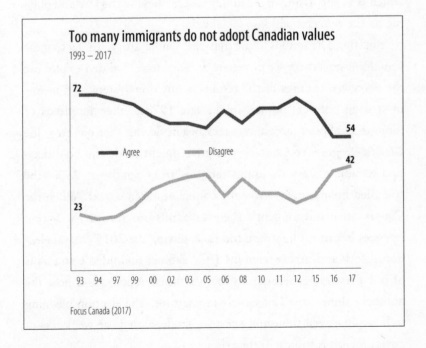

Too many immigrants do not adopt Canadian values
1993 – 2017

72

54

Agree   Disagree

42

23

93   94   97   99   00   02   03   05   06   08   10   11   12   15   16   17

Focus Canada (2017)

Canada's commitment to immigration—expressed in attitudes about traditionally related issues, such as the integrity of the refugee processing system, jobs and the relationship between immigration and crime—is much different from what plays out in the U.S., where Mexican migrants have been accused of importing crime and taking jobs from American citizens.

Since the late 1980s, the majority of Canadians have felt that some refugee claimants are not legitimate. The sentiment was most prevalent in 1987, when 79 per cent agreed with this view. The intervening years have seen a handful of highly publicized incidents when hundreds of refugees or economic migrants arrived by boat under murky circumstances—mainly Tamils arriving in B.C. and Newfoundland. Those incidents did prompt negative responses, which isn't surprising in a country where obeying the law and playing by the rules remain key social values.

But those reactions don't tell the whole story. In fact, most Canadian governments in recent decades have avoided exploiting the perceived failings of the refugee admission system as a means of scoring political points. In the late 1970s, when hundreds of thousands of Vietnamese refugees began fleeing that country, Joe Clark's Progressive Conservative government made the bold decision to admit sixty thousand refugees from Southeast Asia—the so-called boat people—over the course of about a year. When the Conservative government's sluggish admission record for Syrian refugees became a lightning rod issue during the 2015 federal election, Clark and others from his 1979 cabinet reminded Canadians of our previous generosity to the Southeast Asians, and how the numbers alone—the Conservatives went into the election pledging to bring in eleven thousand Syrians—underscored the weakness of government's response to the crisis.

The Vietnamese refugees, according to University of California–Berkeley sociologist Irene Bloemraad, have had great success integrating into Canadian society. By 2016, on the heels of the electoral showdown over the Syrian refugee question, the proportion of those who agreed that some refugees were illegitimate had fallen to 44 per cent, below the proportion of those who disagreed. That trend points to a few conclusions, not least of which is increased public confidence in the federal government institutions responsible for the screening and admissions systems.

We see an almost identical finding when we ask whether the Canadian immigration officials are doing a good job keeping out criminals and suspected criminals. Between 1993 and 2016, public sentiment underwent a complete inversion on this question. In the early 1990s, fewer than three in ten Canadians expressed confidence in the screening system, while 62 per cent suspected that immigration controls weren't keeping criminals out of the country. Today, the figures are reversed: 26 per cent doubt the effectiveness of these controls, while the proportion of those who are satisfied with this aspect of the system has risen steadily, now sitting at 65 per cent.

There's also a fairly broad consensus that immigrants don't contribute to increasing crime. That view is held by only 26 per cent of the population and is most prevalent in Alberta and among those who did not attend college. (Violent crime in most parts of Canada, and in big cities that attract most newcomers, has been dropping for years.)

That outlook contrasts sharply with the view of immigration south of the border, especially among registered Republicans, many of whom have persuaded themselves that immigration and terrorism are the twin scourges destroying America. This negative perception of immigrants also links to the widespread belief that illegal immigrants are responsible for an increase in violent crimes, a connection that has no basis in fact, despite political rhetoric to the contrary. In fact, one analysis showed that urban areas with higher concentrations of immigrants had slightly *lower* property crime rates than other areas. The twenty metropolitan areas with the largest numbers of unauthorized immigrants had noticeably lower rates of property and violent crime than metros generally.[2]

While these views are linked to the obvious historical and geographical differences between Canada and the U.S.—Canada doesn't have as porous a border to fret about, and a narrower legacy of slavery—this divergence is also tied to the way Canada has managed immigration, resettlement, housing, education and the other services geared to newcomers. After all, if most Canadians believe that immigration is benefiting the country both socially and economically at a time when much of the rest of the world has come to precisely the opposite conclusion, something about how Canada is handling this transformation must be working.

THERE WAS A time, of course, when both English and French Canada were neither welcoming nor open-minded. Governments in the late nineteenth and early twentieth centuries sought to curb Chinese immigration with a head tax and then a Chinese exclusion law in 1924. Vancouver experienced riots by thousands of white supremacists and violence directed at Chinese and Japanese immigrants in 1907.[3] In Toronto in 1933, anti-Semitic youth gangs wielding banners covered with swastikas battled Jewish youth in a storied riot at Christie Pits, a downtown ballpark; the incident had been preceded by months of smaller skirmishes, as well as a long campaign by some Torontonians to have Jews banned from the city's beaches. During World War II, the Canadian government interned German- and Japanese-Canadians, as did the U.S. government. And in what's become one of the darkest episodes in Canadian immigration history, federal officials refused to allow a ship carrying German-Jewish refugees to land in Halifax. "None is too many," one internal memo infamously stated.

While immigration levels surged early in the twentieth century, including from non-English-speaking countries, the signal change in Canada's immigration story occurred in the 1960s, when the government moved to make the immigration admission system colour-blind.[4] Credit for this reform, interestingly, is claimed by both the Tories and the Liberals: John Diefenbaker's government enacted a race-blind immigration policy in 1962, but Lester Pearson's Liberals, a few years later, implemented a discrimination-free points system. Since then, immigration from the U.S., Europe and the British Isles has dropped steadily, replaced with growing cohorts of newcomers from the rest of the world.

The next dramatic shift occurred in the 1980s, when the Tory government of Brian Mulroney bumped the annual immigration levels to about 1 per cent of the population, a significant increase meant to address the demographic problem of declining birth rates and an aging population.

While such changes didn't prompt widespread backlash, there's little doubt that the Reform Party movement, which emerged from Alberta in the early 1990s, was fueled in part by anti-immigrant sentiment. The party targeted official multiculturalism as a waste of taxpayer funds while its surrogates, such as the bestselling author William Gairdner (*The Trouble with Canada*), were far more explicit in their denunciation of employment equity and immigration policies that seemed to be changing the country's composition.

In Quebec, meanwhile, separatist and nationalist governments and parties have periodically set their rhetorical sights on these issues. When former Bloc Québécois premier Jacques Parizeau blamed "money and the ethnic vote" for the party's second independence referendum loss in 1995, he was verbalizing a potent undercurrent in the province's attitudes towards newcomers and racialized minorities—attitudes that lingered through more recent debates about "reasonable accommodation" and dress codes for public servants.

None of these sideshows have made much of a dent in immigration levels, however. Today, almost all net population growth in Canada is attributable to immigration. On a per capita basis, Canada's foreign-born population is much larger than the comparable proportion in both the U.S. and most Western European nations, with the bulk of the newcomers settling in large metropolitan areas. The issue of immigration has tended not to be controversial in Canada for many years, and the main political parties are largely in consensus about the importance of immigration for the country's economy and future security.

After all, in an aging society in which the dependency ratio—the proportion of retired people to those in the workforce—is rising quickly, younger newcomers are generally needed to fill job vacancies and take care of the millions of boomers who are exiting the workforce.

Canadians on the whole seem to understand the drivers. Support for maintaining immigration levels actually *rose* during and after the 2009 recession. In most countries, that would be a politically improbable result given the fact that, in times of economic hardship, the finger of blame often points towards the other.

Attitudes towards immigration in the U.S. have a clear geographic context. Greater opposition is concentrated in border areas and de-industrialized regions—where one finds many of the white working-class voters who backed Trump—whereas stronger support for immigrants is found in big cities and along both coasts. By contrast, Canadian opinion tends to be driven more by demographics and social values.

The groups most likely to favour immigration are those with a university education, the young and, interestingly, men. The group least likely to favour Canada's immigration policies is the unemployed. What's more, those who feel that crime is falling, approve of same-sex marriage and generally prefer Canadian over American lifestyles are also more likely to see immigration and multiculturalism as positives and a source of pride.

While we seem to have entered a period where overt expressions of xenophobia or ultranationalism in many Western nations not only find a receptive audience but also attract votes, the reality is that Canadians' views on immigration, especially from nonwhite countries, have already been subjected to numerous tests. Since the early 1990s, we've seen Western populism, Quebec nationalism, periods of sharp economic contraction, terrorist threats and highly publicized refugee controversies. In short, we've experienced some version of "it" already—many times, in fact—but Canadians' core social values continue to embrace diversity and reasonable accommodation.

THAT'S THE RESULT. But the question is, How did we get here? What is it about the way we conduct our politics, manage our services, debate public issues and organize our communities that has produced a conspicuously sturdy national view supporting cultural diversity?

The social processes at play are complex and dynamic, and it would be a mistake to assume that we're somehow morally superior or that each cohort of immigrants welcomes the next one with open arms. The story is actually much more complicated and nuanced, but it is rooted in the sharp divergence between Canadian and American social values that's taken place over the past two decades.

Early in the new millennium, almost six in ten Canadians were of the view that Canadian and American cultures had been converging through the 1990s. That outlook echoed warnings in the late 1980s by anti-free-trade activists who argued that integrating the two economies would force us to eventually abandon the political institutions and values that make Canada distinct. Some said we could even lose Medicare.

But the two cultures were in fact moving in opposite directions. One of the clearest indicators of that trend came from a question that reveals authoritarian beliefs: Asked if the father must be the master of his own house, 49 per cent of Americans agreed in 2000, while only 18 per cent of Canadians did. Americans also tended to be more religious, willing to take risks, aspirational and money focused. They sought a high standard of living, enjoyed put-down humour and believed in a winner-take-all approach to competition. Canadian values, on the other hand, veered in other directions: more secular, risk averse and self-effacing. Canadians believed in income redistribution, compulsory philanthropy (taxes) and a society focused on delivering the best quality of life, not the most income.

That was 2003. In the U.S., the period roughly following the 9/11 attacks (2000–2004) revealed a shift towards "status and security," which means the pursuit of the American dream by following accepted norms and rules, the conviction that such goals can be achieved with a strong work ethic, a desire for material success as a means of demonstrating improved social standing and a belief in traditional institutions and identities. But over the next eight years,

2004 to 2012, we noticed a marked change and a drift towards a greater sense of exclusion and intensity. Americans had a desire to rebuild, but they also had lingering financial insecurity, greater interest in personal empowerment and personal development, and more openness to new relationships and identities.

The immediate post-9/11 period, in other words, was marked by a relatively high degree of national consensus about the prosecution of the wars in Afghanistan and Iraq, coupled with a focus on a common enemy: Al Qaeda. But as the decade and its financial excesses give way to the credit crisis and the ascent to power of America's first African-American president, there arose the beginnings of the social fracturing that found its first expression with the Tea Party movement in 2010, followed by the beginnings of the deep and widening ideological divisions that marked American attitudes about gay marriage, immigration and climate change.

This polarization gained momentum between 2012 and 2016, a period that saw a continued decline in traditional values and support for existing institutions alongside the acceptance of other family forms and, at the same time, growing xenophobia and parochialism, as well as a shift backwards to a more traditional understanding of gender roles.

When we map the changes in American social values between 1992 and 2016, the picture that emerges is one of a society buffeted by its endless disputes (abortion, gun owner's rights, race, the role of government), unceasing terrorism abroad and a devastating attack on their homeland. The picture reveals sharp swings between individuality and authority, and between survival and fulfillment. It is a picture of seemingly permanent flux and polarization, the kind of environment that would allow for a swing in political leadership between two men who could scarcely be more different.

The Canadian social values trajectory is remarkably different. In the twenty-four years from 1992 to 2016, the picture that emerges is of a society that has moved steadily away from values associated with authority and towards those tied to individuality. We see, for example, a shift away from traditional families, gender roles and sexually conservative habits, as well as a declining focus on status, consumption and material goods. There's greater support for activist government and, relevant to immigration, a more globalist outlook.

Canadians' attitude towards violence—and the idea that sometimes violent behaviour can serve as a way of releasing tension—shows another sharp difference. Canadians have a lower threshold for violence and are far less likely to agree with the statement that "It's no big deal" to blow off stress with an outburst (17 per cent to 10 per cent). This finding offers some insights into the vitriol and anger that characterized the 2016 U.S. presidential election—crowds calling for Hillary Clinton's imprisonment as well as cheering when Trump invoked the way protesters were dealt with in the "old days."

In sum, the trajectory of Canadian values shows a society whose priorities have evolved steadily towards an open, progressive outlook that recognizes diversity, the positive role of government and alternative ways of living.

THE STORY OF Canada's outlook on immigration and multiculturalism is embedded within this broader evolution in our social values, but it also has contributed to the shift in what Canadians view as important. It's a mutually reinforcing process, a virtuous cycle.

Consider trade, for example. While Canada's economy has traditionally depended on exports, especially raw materials as well as goods manufactured in Ontario and Quebec, the federal government's push in the late 1980s for reduced tariffs and import controls was met with opposition from both Liberals and the NDP. Almost three decades later, serious opposition to free-trade deals has melted, and Canadians seem to accept efforts by their governments to forge improved economic ties with Latin America, the Asia-Pacific nations, India and Europe. Yet the growing public consensus around globalized trade occurred during a period when immigrant entrepreneurs from these regions began to play a broader role in financing or orchestrating that trade or building businesses that catered to newcomer communities.

Education is another sphere where there's evidence of a self-reinforcing dynamic in Canada's experience with immigration. In the late 1990s, Canada switched its points-based immigration admissions policy to one that places an emphasis on skills, education, language and capital (as well as family re-unification). As a result, a growing proportion of newcomers have arrived with postsecondary degrees.

Numerous studies, including those conducted by the federal government,[5] have shown that immigrants have, on average, higher postsecondary educational attainment than Canadian-born residents. More recent newcomers are even better educated than previous ones, with many packing much coveted business and engineering degrees in their suitcases. In fact, as University of Toronto immigration expert Jeffrey Reitz has shown, the proportion of immigrants with bachelor's degrees has *nearly doubled* from about 25 per cent in the early 1990s to about 45 per cent since 2001. This is, or at least should be, a good-news story.

The story of immigrant education levels has many tendrils, but there's no doubt that Canada's policy decision to attract newcomers with marketable skills and higher education reinforces the prevailing views about the importance of immigration and its role in the country's economic well-being. Anyone who believes Canada's policy is altruistic or humanitarian or reveals our moral superiority should look again: by targeting people who are more likely to succeed economically and thus place less of a strain on the social safety net, Ottawa has opted to pursue national economic goals that have social and cultural benefits.

There's a big payoff in terms of public opinion, as we've found in our social values surveys. A consistent theme is that those with more education are more likely to hold favourable views about newcomers and diversity. As well, the children of immigrants with postsecondary education are themselves more likely to pursue higher education. In short, the current points system effectively fosters a self-reinforcing cycle, with educated children of educated immigrants supporting a policy that encourages Canada to continue attracting educated immigrants.

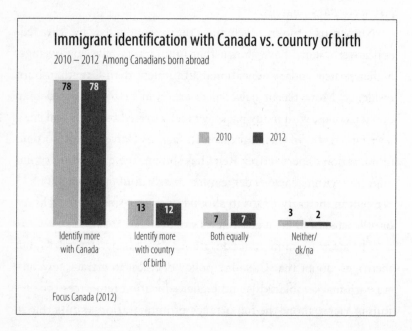

Immigrant identification with Canada vs. country of birth

2010 – 2012 Among Canadians born abroad

2010   2012

	2010	2012
Identify more with Canada	78	78
Identify more with country of birth	13	12
Both equally	7	7
Neither/dk/na	3	2

Focus Canada (2012)

Jeffrey Reitz points out that in France, a much larger proportion of Muslim immigrants have attained only a high school degree or less. The French earn their anti-immigration reputation in part because they complain so vocally that the North Africans living in social housing in the suburbs of their big cities drain public coffers. By contrast, Canada's national conversation about immigrants is mostly positive because we have accepted the belief that university-educated immigrants are good for the economy.

But the good-news story of highly educated immigrants finding opportunity in Canada—and in return helping bear the costs of hip replacements and home care for aging boomers—is not the whole story. Indeed, upward mobility for immigrants to Canada began to falter in the early 1990s and remains stagnant, and immigrant children say they face more prejudice and discrimination than their parents did. "Is it possible," Dr. Reitz wonders pointedly, "that the situation of Canadian immigrants (or at least some categories of Canadian immigrants) and the attitudes of Canadians towards immigration are less rosy than many of us are prepared to believe?"

The evidence I have seen on Canadian inclusivity leads me to a glass that is both half empty and half full.

Wen-Hao Chen and Feng Hou of Statistics Canada have compared second-generation immigrant groups to those whose families have been in Canada three generations or more. White immigrants do as well as those here three generations or more in terms of educational attainment, employment rates, occupational attainment and income. Almost all other groups (Chinese, South Asian, Japanese, West Asian, Arab and Korean) have either the same or better educational attainment as those here three generations or more, but almost all groups do either the same or less well than three-generation-plus Canadians when it comes to employment rates, occupational status and earnings.

Those with Filipino backgrounds do significantly worse when it comes to occupational status and earnings. Those whose parents came from West Asian and Middle Eastern countries and Korea suffer lower employment rates and below-average earnings. And worst off are those second-generation groups who are black or come from Latin America. Their occupational status is below and their earnings are far below those of three-plus-generation Canadians. When looking at these disparate economic outcomes for equally qualified people, one can only conclude that racialized groups are victims of varying degrees of discrimination and racism. That's an undeniable problem.

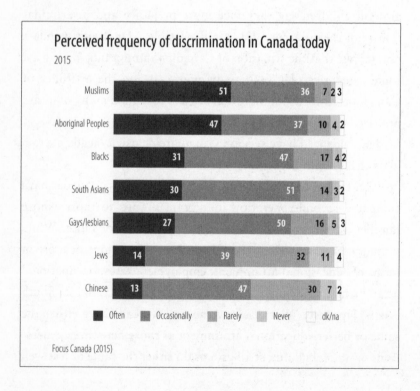

Focus Canada (2015)

The glass-half-full side of the story is the fact that most Canadians acknowledge that there is discrimination against various groups. Well over three-quarters of Canadians tell us that Muslims often or occasionally suffer from discrimination. Similar proportions say the same happens to Indigenous Canadians and only slightly fewer say that blacks and South Asians are also often or occasionally victims of discrimination. As the saying goes, the first step towards getting better is recognizing that you have a problem.

CHAPTER FOUR

On Being Muslim in Canada— Optimism with Vigilance

The closing weeks of the 2016 Canadian federal election saw the collision of two highly charged issues that cut close to some of the core values Canadians hold dear. As the long campaign churned towards a decision point, the country became riveted by a tragedy on a faraway beach and the Canadian government's role, however tenuous, in allowing it to happen.

In early September, a photographer snapped an image of tiny Alan Kurdi, a three-year-old boy of Syrian Kurdish origin who'd drowned on one of the perilous crossings being made by tens of thousands of refugees fleeing the violence in Syria. Over the next several days, the media reported that the Kurdi family had sought asylum in Canada but had been turned down. "Yes, the authorities in Canada, which rejected my application for asylum, even though there were five families who were willing to support us financially," Alan's father told a German newspaper.[1]

The Kurdis' immigration story turned out to be complicated, but the revelation sent a shock wave through the election, which had seen opposition parties accuse the Harper government of failing to meet its own refugee targets for Syrians fleeing the war. With

Canadian reporters now showing footage directly from the Syrians' exodus journeys across Europe, thousands of people began banding together to form refugee sponsorship groups to assist the fleeing Syrians. Trudeau and NDP leader Thomas Mulcair both pledged to boost the admission targets if elected.

While Syrian refugees faced violence in countries like Hungary and became a prop for Republican presidential candidates stoking Americans' fears of Islamic terrorism, many Canadians seemed to be heading in the opposite direction.[2]

The outpouring coincided with a pivotal legal development in the long-running controversy over niqabs. That debate played out at the end of a campaign that had come to focus on the stance that the federal government should adopt on issues that cut close to the way many Canadians conceptualize themselves—tolerant, welcoming to immigrants and respectful of all religions, provided the practitioners are law-abiding.

Zunera Ishaq, a teacher who came to Canada from Pakistan in 2008, had challenged a federal law requiring those taking the oath of citizenship to show their faces. Ishaq, who wore a niqab that covered her face, challenged the law as unconstitutional. She agreed to remove her veil in a private session so female citizenship officials could confirm her identity, but she declined to do so during the public ceremony, citing her right to observe her own religious practices. During a leadership debate in early October, the party leaders jousted over the law, which traces its roots to the long-standing political debate in Quebec about measures that would ban religious clothing from the public sphere, such as government offices and classrooms.

The Harper government believed it had public opinion on its side, thanks in part to a poll conducted for the Privy Council

Office (which reports to the Prime Minister's Office) in March 2015 by Leger Marketing. The results showed that 82 per cent of Canadians across the country oppose allowing women to wear the niqab during citizenship ceremonies. The media treated the finding as conclusive.

Just two weeks before Election Day, however, the Federal Court of Appeal ruled in Ishaq's favour, and she took the oath of citizenship a few days later in a highly charged political environment. "It actually confirmed my belief in the justice system of . . . Canada," she told the CBC after the ceremony.[3]

IN THE MONTHS following, media commentators in the U.S. and the U.K. marveled at the deluge of offers of sponsorship by Canadians of Syrian refugees, even as that phrase itself had become part of Trump's rallying cry for halting Muslim immigration in the name of national security. What's more, the apparent disdain that many Canadians expressed about the niqab, and all it represented, wasn't especially evident on Election Day, when the majority of Canadian voters seemed to reject the tone of policies that had a distinctly anti-Muslim ring.

Did we get to this juncture out of some kind of heightened sense of moral enlightenment about the role of Muslims in Canadian society? As with many of these issues, the answer is nuanced, even though these episodes do reveal how Canadian attitudes towards multiculturalism and immigration have become increasingly consolidated over the course of a generation.

The public response to the Harper government's policies on issues such as refugees and head coverings suggests that Canadians are keenly aware of the obstacles that some Muslims face today. According to our surveys, 87 per cent of Canadians said that Muslims are often or occasionally the targets of racism. (Muslims, in fact, were seen as the group most likely to experience bigotry, with Indigenous people coming a close second, at 84 per cent.) What's more, Canadians' awareness of the existence of these attitudes has grown. In 2015, fifty-one per cent said Muslims were "often" subjected to discrimination, up from 43 per cent in 2006.

This shift is significant, given that it occurred during a period when the Arab Spring of 2009 gave way to the brutal civil war in Syria, the explosion of Islamic State–sponsored violence and the refugee crisis. The period was also marked by aggressive international recruiting efforts by ISIS, horrific executions and a stream of wrenching news about terrorist attacks in Western cities, including Boston, Brussels, Paris and London.

There's no disputing that Muslims living in the West have experienced a sharp backlash. Populist politicians in France, Germany, the Netherlands and Hungary have lashed out against Muslim minorities while Trump sought to ban immigration from six Muslim-majority countries. In the U.S., according to the Pew Center, reported incidents of hate crimes against Muslims jumped 67 per cent between 2014 and 2015, and have reached post-9/11 levels.[4] In the immediate aftermath of the U.S. presidential election, civil liberties groups reported a noticeable spike in anti-Muslim, anti-black, anti-LGBTQ+, anti-Semitic and anti-immigrant incidents.[5]

Canada hasn't been immune to those sentiments. According to various media reports, anti-Muslim incidents rose between 2012 and 2014, even as the frequency of hate crimes overall dropped. In Mississauga, Ontario, some homeowners launched a campaign in 2015 to halt the construction of a large mosque; the ostensible reasons involved concerns about traffic and parking, but the group's anti-Muslim rhetoric suggested an ulterior motive. More recently, anti-Muslim protesters picketed a downtown Toronto mosque and shouted hateful slogans during a school board meeting in the suburb of Brampton when trustees were considering the logistics of in-school Friday prayers for Muslim students.[6] One demonstrator went so far as to tear up a copy of the Qur'an and toss it on the floor of the school board council chamber. Peel school board officials hastened to gather the torn pages and return them—a gesture "the whole community really appreciated," a local imam said.[7]

The most virulent anti-Muslim act, however, occurred on January 29, 2017, when a man burst into a local mosque and killed six people, all Muslims.[8] Alexandre Bissonnette, a Quebec City man known as an online troll and an admirer of the French ultranationalist leader Marine Le Pen, was charged with six counts of first degree and five of attempted murder. As of the time of writing, a trial had not yet taken place and Bissonnette hadn't entered a plea to the allegations.

ONE MEASURE OF the status of Muslims in Canadian society is how the members of this small and extended community perceive their own role and sense of security in a world that seems fixated on their religious practices.

The evolving response to the use of head coverings offers some important insights. A decade ago, Mario Dumont's Action Démocratique du Québec, which vaulted to official opposition status in the 2007 Quebec election, pushed provincial lawmakers to debate "reasonable accommodation" policies that could have prevented public servants from wearing head coverings. Meanwhile, the media was paying close attention to the case of a hijab-wearing teenage girl who'd been ejected from a soccer game because the scarf apparently posed a safety risk.

Despite the play such stories received, only 42 per cent of Canadian Muslim women wore hijabs, and just 3 per cent wore the more extensive coverings, like burkas or niqabs. What's more, 57 per cent of Muslims wanted to adopt Canadian customs and another 13 per cent sought to adopt Canadian customs yet remain culturally distinctive. Muslims are overwhelmingly proud to be Canadians and express dedication to the sorts of values that are common throughout society at large (freedom and democracy, multiculturalism, peacefulness, humanitarianism). And while Muslims living in Canada in the mid-2000s faced challenges around discrimination and employment, they nonetheless expressed pride to be in Canada and felt their coreligionists were safer here than in other Western nations.

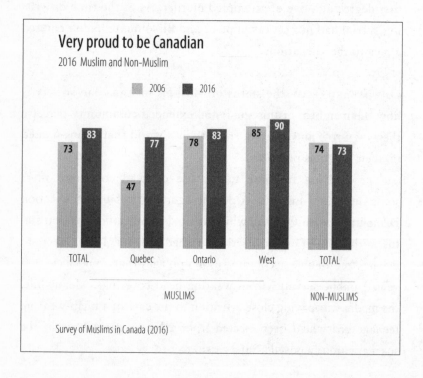

Very proud to be Canadian
2016 Muslim and Non-Muslim

2006   2016

	2006	2016
TOTAL (Muslims)	73	83
Quebec	47	77
Ontario	78	83
West	85	90
TOTAL (Non-Muslims)	74	73

MUSLIMS   NON-MUSLIMS

Survey of Muslims in Canada (2016)

That sense of identification with the country and its dominant social values has grown over the past decade. In 2016, 83 per cent of Muslims in Canada were proud to be Canadian, up from 73 per cent in 2006. The growth in that sense of Canadian identity has been especially pronounced in Quebec (77 per cent compared to 47 per cent in 2006), and finds its highest levels in Western Canada, where 90 per cent of Muslims report pride in their citizenship. Interestingly, those levels are higher than among non-Muslims overall (73 per cent).

Muslims in Canada are also increasingly optimistic about the country's direction—89 per cent expressed optimism in 2016, compared to 81 per cent in 2006—and are more upbeat than Canadians generally. Overall, when asked to name the most important values that immigrants should adopt in order to be good citizens, Muslims and other Canadians generally agree in their responses: fluency in English or French (23 per cent among Muslims, compared to 26 per cent overall), tolerance and respect for others (19 per cent compared to 15 per cent overall), and respect for Canadian history and culture (17 per cent compared to 22 per cent generally). Over half said they want to adopt Canadian customs, and the proportion that indicated a desire to remain distinct fell to 17 per cent from 23 per cent over the past decade, a finding that suggests a growing desire by Muslim immigrants and their children to integrate.

The way Muslims in Canada perceive discrimination against their own communities is also trending in directions that corroborate these other trends.

You don't need to be a psychologist or sociologist to understand the relationship between a drumbeat of negative political messaging about a visible minority group and its own sense of vulnerability. In the run-up to the March 2016 elections in the Netherlands, Geert

Wilders pledged to close mosques, ban the Qur'an, end Muslim immigration and de-Islamize the country.[9] As Al Jazeera reported before the vote, a recent government report showed that 40 per cent of Dutch Muslims were no longer comfortable in the country. "Even if I'm born here," one said, "I don't feel at home."[10]

What's more, showy edicts—such as Trump's executive orders suspending travel from six Muslim-majority countries—send a clear signal that partisan goals take precedence over the sorts of freedoms that most people take for granted, such as international travel or having relatives visit from abroad.

On occasion, Canadian politicians have let loose with public pronouncements that sent a clear signal about how they think Muslims should conduct themselves. In 2007, the council of Hérouxville, a small Quebec town, passed a code saying that new immigrants should avoid controversial conduct, including covering their faces entirely and stoning women. The move brought international media attention, and the municipality a few years later began thinking about dropping the code because it had caused residents so much embarrassment.[11] But with the exception of the Harper government's Barbaric Cultural Practices act and hotline, anti-Muslim politics at the federal level in Canada have tended to be far less explicit and shrouded in euphemisms about national security concerns.

Why the caution? Is it because Canadian politicians are simply better people, less inclined to score political points by preying on the anxieties of the most frightened or hostile voters? Unlikely. Politicians everywhere want to fish where the fishing's good, as the saying goes. Rather, and more likely, those who are tempted to tap into anti-Muslim sentiment here—to throw some red meat or a wink to an anti-immigrant constituency—also know they need to be careful with such messaging for fear of alienating other voting blocs. Muslims still make up only a tiny proportion of the population, just 3.2 per cent across Canada, with higher proportions in Greater Toronto (7.25 per cent) and Montreal (6 per cent), according to the 2011 National Household Survey.[12] But other newcomer groups, as well as the kind of urban liberals who sponsor refugees, may identify with them and quickly pick up on attempts to isolate or target them.

The latter interpretation would explain another important shift in relations between this minority community and the wider society. In 2006, when Muslim Canadians were asked to estimate how many other Canadians held hostile views about those who come from their religious tradition, more than half chose "many" or "just some," while only 35 per cent said "very few." A decade later, however, 49 per cent of Muslims in Canada chose "very few," and fewer now perceive higher levels of hostility. In short, Muslims themselves seem to see less hostility in the society around them than they did a decade ago.

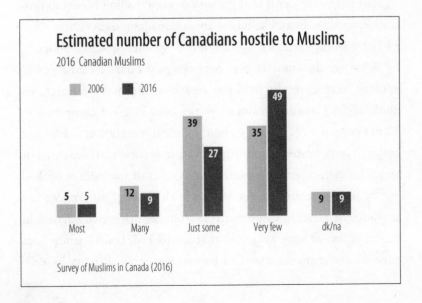

Estimated number of Canadians hostile to Muslims
2016 Canadian Muslims

2006   2016

Most: 5, 5
Many: 12, 9
Just some: 39, 27
Very few: 35, 49
dk/na: 9, 9

Survey of Muslims in Canada (2016)

This change, incidentally, isn't happening in an environment in which Muslims have stopped worrying about discrimination and the way they are treated generally, which remains, as of 2016, the most top-of-mind concern facing these individuals in their own communities.

It's not an unfounded concern. In the wake of the Quebec City mass shooting in January 2017, Mississauga, Ontario, Liberal backbencher MP Iqra Khalid tabled a motion in the House of Commons calling on the government to "condemn Islamophobia and all forms of systemic racism and religious discrimination." Despite that tragedy, the motion, known as M-103, triggered something of a backlash, with some well-publicized polls showing it enjoys the support of less than 50 per cent of the public. If Canadians are not in denial about the existence of anti-Muslim discrimination, what would explain the hesitant public response to a motion to tackle that precise problem?

Part of the answer is that it's easy to skew polling results to generate a headline. In all likelihood, most Canadians didn't know what M-103 was, or whether it was a symbolic gesture or actual policy.

What we do know is that over the past quarter century, Canadians have generally held the view that too many immigrants don't adopt Canadian values (54 per cent in 2017 compared to 72 per cent in 1993). Worry about cultural integration is stronger among Conservative supporters than it is among Canadians at large. Indeed, when we examine the values of Canadians broken out by party preference, discomfort with cultural differences is a key point separating Conservatives from the other two parties. In recent years we have also seen that a backlash constituency does exist—a constituency alarmed by some aspects of living in a diverse society and affronted that they are not permitted to air their alarm without being labelled racists.

Yet Muslims, and Muslim women in particular, may be benefiting from countervailing cultural trends, for example, the growing importance Canadians assign to gender equality, which is now our most important aspirational value.

The connection may seem counterintuitive. After all, one of the most common criticisms of Islamic tradition is that some observant women wear head scarves or hijabs, a gesture that appears to some critics as evidence of an unequal or submissive relationship with men. That, certainly, was one of the arguments the Harper government used to justify banning niqabs in certain public settings. But, as University of Toronto sociologist Jeffrey Reitz pointed out about Zunera Ishaq's legal challenge to this rule, she countered the law from a feminist position, noting in interviews that her husband actually didn't favour her decision to cover her face. "I am not looking for Mr. Harper to approve my life choices or dress," Ishaq wrote in a *Toronto Star* op-ed. "I am certainly not looking for him to speak on my behalf and 'save' me from oppression."

Many Canadians worry that not all women who wear niqabs are so empowered. Yet Ishaq's assertions of independence likely found a receptive audience among younger Canadians. No student who has set foot in a Canadian postsecondary institution in recent years would be surprised to see many young women wearing hijabs; it is a perfectly common sight (niqabs and burkas, less so). As with LGBTQ+ rights and attitudes towards immigrants generally, millennials demonstrate a degree of openness to difference that is markedly different from their parents' generation.

Consumer trends are also having an impact. A decade ago, teenage girls playing soccer were told to remove hijabs for safety reasons. Today, fashion and sports equipment giants like Nike and Hummel, a Danish firm, are marketing hijabs, sensing a growing market of young customers who seem more empowered than oppressed. "With sensitivities over immigration and the perceived threat of Muslim extremism running high, the head scarf has led to attacks against Muslim women," Reuters noted when Nike launched its Pro Hijab this spring. "At the same time, the hijab has evolved as a symbol of diversity that Nike has embraced."[13]

Some of these products have triggered surreal episodes. In the summer of 2016, French police busied themselves with forcing Muslim women to remove so-called burkinis at beaches packed with bikini-clad (or topless) sun worshippers. News reports of this spectacle highlighted both the ridiculousness and the irony of cops enforcing female dress codes ostensibly meant to protect women from oppression.

Canadians, however, have already figured out how to make their peace with articles of clothing closely associated with non-Christian religious traditions. In the late 1980s and early 1990s, a handful of Canadian followers of the Sikh religion sought the right to wear a beard and the traditional turban in work or institutional settings. Baltej Singh Dhillon, a Malaysian-born man who immigrated to British Columbia in 1983, applied to join the RCMP in 1988. Bound by religious observance to wear the turban and a beard, Dhillon asked for special dispensation and eventually decided to challenge the Mounties' dress code. While opposition was strident and took a racist turn, Brian Mulroney's Progressive Conservative government in 1990 changed the rules, allowing Dhillon to embark on a law enforcement career.

The Canadian Human Rights Commission, the Federal Court and the Supreme Court of Canada all upheld this decision.[14] At that time, 70 per cent of Canadians opposed such accommodation (59 per cent of them were strongly opposed). Once the courts ruled that turbans were, in fact, permissible by law, most Canadians quickly accepted these judgments.

Today, law enforcement agencies across Canada employ turban-wearing police officers. There are numerous Sikh Canadians who hold elected office, including Harjit Sajjan, the Liberal defense minister, and Jagmeet Singh, a Brampton, Ontario, NDP MPP who declared his candidacy for the leadership of the federal wing of his party in May 2017. So it's hardly surprising that the RCMP last summer announced that it was further tweaking its uniform policy, allowing female officers to wear hijabs.[15] Other police services, such as Peel Region's, have followed suit.

Condemning France's burkini bans as "discriminatory, counter-productive and divisive," Postmedia guest editorialist Harvey Enchin noted the contrast in national responses. "The difference is stark: as police in Canada reach out to Muslim women, police in France shame and marginalize them."

The lack of public outrage about the RCMP's move suggests that public opinion in Canada is following the same script that played out with Sikh turbans in the early 1990s: controversy and backlash, legal challenges, and then growing public acceptance of a judicial result. So while the Harper Conservatives may have felt that they had public opinion at their backs when they sought to ban face coverings at citizenship hearings based on a single snapshot, the picture turned out to be more complex than they reckoned. It appears that Canadians can express negative opinions out of fear or misunderstanding in an instant poll on a controversial topic. But upon reflection and after some public debate and perhaps a legal judgment, they come to a different attitude rooted in their values and the better angels of their nature.

We do a grave disservice to the Muslim community and to all Canadians if we rush to conclude that our country is less tolerant of religious diversity than in fact may be the case. Perhaps it is for this reason that the niqab didn't prove to have the traction that some may have hoped for and others had feared.

CHAPTER FIVE

The Taxi Driver with the PhD

In the mid-2000s, a handful of big cities in France and England experienced violent race riots. Police in the predominantly immigrant suburbs of London and Paris battled with young men, many of them of North African descent. These showdowns occurred in isolated public housing projects inhabited mainly by visible minority immigrants who had been shunted to the urban edges, cut off from decent jobs, humane housing, open space and the prospect of a comfortable future.

The worst of these began on October 27, 2005, after the deaths of two young men fleeing from police in the Paris *banlieue* of Clichy-sous-Bois. The riots, which spread throughout France, smoldered for almost three weeks, caused millions of euros in damage and prompted the French government to impose a state of emergency. Similar unrest broke out in a London suburb a few years later, and such incidents have occurred with some regularity, if not comparable ferocity, ever since.

The news of how grinding suburban disaffection had ignited widespread rioting did not escape the notice of members of racial minority and newcomer communities living in the suburban housing projects in parts of Toronto. "There's a possibility of it happening here," Razad Khan, an eighteen-year-old from the San Romanoway complex at Jane Street and Finch Avenue, told *The Globe and Mail* in 2005.[1] "That's how we feel about it. It could be a threat."

Other analysts began pondering the same question: Are Canada's versions of the French *banlieues* ticking time bombs, filled with marginalized and volatile resentment? As the noted urbanist Richard Florida wrote in the wake of another round of rioting (in London in the run-up to the 2012 Olympics): "Until we acknowledge our growing class divisions, they are only going to get worse. And if the time comes that they do bubble over, as they just did in London, we won't be able to say we weren't warned."[2]

Florida, an American urban studies theorist now at the University of Toronto, brought the term "creative class" into common parlance. He was referring to a growing body of Canadian research showing a long-term dynamic that is redrawing the face of our largest urban centres. Sociologist David Hulchanski has developed the "Three Cities" maps that reveal the gradual changes in the location and size of the lower-, middle- and upper-income neighbourhoods in Toronto, Vancouver and Montreal.[3] The analysis vividly reveals the geography of income polarization, and the way these cities, once defined by a proliferation of mixed-income neighbourhoods, are increasingly sorting themselves into self-contained enclaves delineated by wealth, race and access to rapid transit, leading to spaces with greater inequality and more rigid divisions.

In one zone, affluent, white, urban-minded residents live in compact leafy neighbourhoods with eye-popping real estate values, plenty of rapid transit service and easy access to the cultural playgrounds downtown. They're centred on funky retail strips with hipster boutiques, upscale bistros, high-end food stores and indie coffee shops.

In another, newcomers and visible minorities rent apartments in aging slab apartment buildings that front onto busy suburban arterials served by overcrowded city buses. Instead of lively retail strips, these areas depend on Walmarts and extended stretches of strip malls packed with small shops and professional services catering to various ethnocultural communities. The postwar single-family residential enclaves in these areas have also become expensive, but they lack the kind of brand value that comes with addresses in the "cooler" parts of the city.

These two sets of neighbourhoods have come to exemplify the twenty-first century's equivalent of Canada's two solitudes—communities whose residents share a city but interact with one another less and less.

Hulchanski's maps, which first focused on the City of Toronto, showed how the face of the city had evolved between 1970 and 2005. At the beginning of that period, much of the city, including the postwar suburbs, could be classified as middle or slightly upper income (Hulchanski used quintiles of average annual income, calculated across census tracts), and neighbourhoods with a concentration of low- or very-low-income residents were clustered downtown or in the swathes of working-class areas that today are experiencing extreme gentrification.

By 2005, however, these income heat maps looked very different, with large chunks of the inner suburbs (Etobicoke, Scarborough, North York) dominated by low-income neighbourhoods. The wealthiest—where average income has grown 20 per cent or more since 1970—were clustered around the subway corridors. The middle-class neighbourhoods—where income has been relatively stable—had shrunk significantly, while the areas that had seen de-clining income expanded dramatically. According to Hulchanski, two-thirds of the city's neighbourhoods in 1970 were middle class, but that figure dropped to 29 per cent by 2005. The poorest and wealthiest neighbourhoods had one thing in common, though: by 2005, there were many more of each.

In this breakdown, areas with more poor residents have lower ed-ucation levels, fewer white-collar jobs, more tenants, lower property values and more people whose housing costs put them in a position of precarity (spending over 30 per cent of monthly take-home income on rent). They are, moreover, areas in which well-paying, unionized manufacturing jobs have been replaced by low-paying service sector or retail positions, many of them part-time shift work.

Through the Neighbourhood Change Project, other academ-ics have extended this analysis to eight major metropolitan areas across Canada.[4] They've put meat on the bones of the Three Cities work, documenting not only the rise of the low-income, immi-grant-dense postwar suburb but also the emergence of so-called ethnoburbs, such as Brampton, Markham, Richmond and Burn-aby, all of which have very large and populous concentrations of East Asians or South Asians, as well as areas with clusters of im-migrants who are falling behind.

The residents of these latter areas have relatively high educa-tion levels but, as Hulchanski notes, employment as managers and professionals remained relatively low in 2006. "The incidence of persons with a degree and in managerial and professional occu-pations declined relative to other clusters. While the percentage of high-income households increased somewhat, the percentage of low-income households increased substantially from 9.1% to 17.9%."[5]

The employment profile of these communities does vary. There are certainly large and growing areas in these cities with significant concentrations of businesses that are run by and employ newcomers and visible minorities. The low-wage service economy also depends heavily on newcomers, visible minorities and the growing cohort of individuals admitted to Canada as temporary foreign workers.

Yet in the public consciousness, the embodiment of the under-employed newcomer has been distilled into the almost mythic figure of the taxi (or Uber) driver with his PhD. These individuals, who are overwhelmingly nonwhite, exemplify what one scholar has described as Canada's "foreign credentials gap."

The highly skilled taxi driver, as it turns out, is not a myth. A recent federal study found that about 44 per cent of Canada's taxi drivers—which is to say, the ones the government actually knows about—have postsecondary degrees or higher, and "may be over-qualified for their jobs." As of the 2006 census, in fact, fully 3.5 per cent of Canada's fifty thousand cabbies had a master's, PhD or medical degree. One, who came here from a developing-world country, drove me to a speaking gig in Calgary, saying he was not unhappy to be driving a taxi in Canada because he was so proud of his kids in university. This man looked forward to going back home to practice medicine during his holidays.

On its own, this finding would be little more than a curiosity. But there's a growing body of evidence to show that while Canada has focused for years on bringing in immigrants with a higher education and specific technical skills, many are underemployed and languish in jobs that fail to take advantage of their training: ophthalmologists working as optometrists' assistants or engineers who can't get their credentials recognized and end up working as technicians or programmers.

As StatsCan reported in 2010, the "education-to-job mismatch is particularly prevalent among recent immigrants with university education." The report noted an analysis of 2006 census data which showed that just 24 per cent of employed foreign-educated, university-level immigrants were working in a regulated occupation that matched their field of study, compared to 62 per cent of their Canadian-born counterparts. "And among immigrants whose occupation did not match their field of study," the report added, "77% worked in jobs that do not usually require a degree, compared to 57% of 'unmatched' Canadian-born graduates."[6]

These findings reinforce the conclusions of other assessments, which show that more recent cohorts of immigrants to Canada, many from developing-world nations, are taking longer to reach the average family income levels for Canadians. Whereas postwar immigrants, many of whom came from Europe, "caught up" to their Canadian-born neighbours relatively quickly, many newer arrivals have struggled. That's due to a range of interconnected factors: the decline of stable manufacturing jobs, language barriers, regulatory obstacles from professional organizations and inadequate settlement services and, let's be frank, systemic racism. In other words, the Canadian social mobility dream, such as it was, may increasingly be an intergenerational aspiration, or, to put it less politely, a bit of a bait-and-switch game.

These mounting concerns, of course, go directly to the question of attaining a stable or prosperous quality of life in Canada; after all, discrimination represents a formidable impediment to a satisfying career. Of 458 Canadian Muslims between the ages of 18 and 34 surveyed, "more than half identify the economy or unemployment as a primary concern for both themselves and their fellow Canadians. These concerns are similarly important to Muslims aged 35 and older."[7]

For certain communities, the obstacles have proved to be especially formidable. Black residents in some lower-income areas experience intensive policing and racial profiling, and most face discrimination.

Somali-Canadians, many of whom arrived as refugees, have also experienced high levels of violent or gang-related crime (in both Toronto and Alberta) and unemployment, despite a desire to integrate into Canadian society.[8] About seventy thousand Somali refugees came to Canada in the early 1990s, and the population of this community has doubled since, with most clustered in Toronto's "Little Mogadishu" neighbourhood in northwest Toronto, as well as in Ottawa and a few other cities. To deal with the aftershocks of war and flight, women in these communities worked to re-establish Somali traditions in a diasporic setting.

From her interviews, the researcher Rima Berns-McGown came across a revealing discrepancy: Being Canadian for these young people means having opportunities that they wouldn't have had in Somalia. But, most fascinatingly, and almost universally, they told Berns-McGowan that being Canadian means being accepting of others, even if you don't agree with them. She said they made this assertion over and over again, regardless of their background, socio-economic status or level of religious observance.

At the same time, respondents did not always believe that other Canadians saw them as Canadian or accepted them as such, and they described encountering both colour racism and Islamophobia. This racism took different forms, including teachers assuming that they would not be able to cope with university or succeed as professionals.

Surveys show that Canadians, though strongly supportive of immigration, nonetheless believe that too many newcomers don't adopt Canadian customs and values. Yet new Canadians tell us they do wish to integrate but they face many barriers, including the prejudices and stereotypes held by the majority of the native-born.

THE EVOLVING FACE of urban Canada is directly pertinent to the broader question of whether Canada is vulnerable to the appeal of nativism. The country's six largest cities are now home to half of Canada's entire population, and they are also experiencing the fastest population growth (7.6 per cent between 2011 and 2016), largely due to immigration. Over 80 per cent of all visible minorities in Canada live in those urban regions, representing just less than half their populations (60 per cent of the residents in those six metros are first- or second-generation Canadians).

It might seem like an obvious conclusion that if the bulk of Canada's population growth is increasingly concentrated in six metropolitan regions that are attractive to newcomers and that tend to be more socially tolerant than medium-sized cities or rural areas, then numbers alone might suggest that Canada can resist the sort of racially inflected populism that has gripped America's red states. But ethnocultural diversity on its own isn't necessarily a bulwark against intolerance. Some newcomer groups have socially conservative traditions that conflict with more liberal mainstream values. As well, acceptance of immigrants depends on other factors, such as access to labour markets, decent schools and adequate housing, all of which prevent the formation of the sort of impoverished high-rise ghettos that ring many major European cities.

In fact, the trends Hulchanski identifies do raise questions about the future social cohesiveness in urban Canada. After all, if these population centres become systematically more spatially segregated by race and class, there are fewer opportunities for meaningful social interaction and integration. In this scenario, all the children in the classroom are the same colour and come from families with similar economic means. Sidewalks, restaurants, libraries and other social spaces become similarly monochromatic. And given that homes close to subway stops have seen some of the sharpest increases in real estate values, one could predict that the visible evidence of sorting may even be apparent on transit vehicles.

Hulchanski warns of the long-term consequences of these urban dynamics, which, he says, hold out the risk of "a more unequal and polarized Canada" where there's little room for either middle-class or mixed-income neighbourhoods. Maybe we won't experience a depressing sequence of rioting, as in London or Paris. But these segregated cities might become harder places to manage, as communities that don't engage with one another are far less likely to agree on public services or policies designed to straddle socioeconomic and geographic boundaries.

There's little evidence to date that public policy in Canada is drifting in a direction that reinforces or exacerbates these changes. For example, planning policy tends to discourage the development of gated communities, which operate outside municipal jurisdiction, maintain secure perimeters and are seen by many critics as heightening social or racial divisions. It's true that there are some examples in suburban or exurban areas across Canada, but the phenomenon never took off in the way it did in the U.S. (According to the most recent estimates from the early 2000s, more than eleven million Americans live in gated communities, whose residents are protected by armed security guards and hard perimeters, and are subject to strict internal rules and regulations. Residential developers reported that eight in ten new homes are built in gated communities, and that in cities like Phoenix, 12 per cent of the population lives in such enclaves.[9])

In terms of public institutions, the Edelman Trust Barometer also shows that Canadians tend not to harbour corrosive levels of distrust or skepticism about government services, which means voters' appetite for radical political programs that call for dramatic solutions—deep tax cuts, major funding shifts—don't have much purchase here. We consistently rank high on global happiness indices, which also explains the electorate's interest in stability and consistency in government.

Social policies with broad reach continue to enjoy public support. The Canada Pension Plan is a good example. Successive reforms, including rate hikes, have helped many seniors avoid poverty, and the creation of the Canada Pension Plan Investment Board by the Chrétien government in the 1990s placed the CPP on stable financial footing. It's true that the Harper Conservatives resisted calls for shoring up the system in advance of the wave of boomer retirements, and some business stakeholder groups complained about higher payroll deductions. But Ottawa has made the necessary changes with little pushback from voters and grudging acceptance from the business sector.

Health care is another example. Canada's universal health system consistently ranks as the most important symbol of national identity, at 88 per cent. Whereas a generation ago, Reform politicians and Conservatives in both Quebec and Alberta pushed for an end to the single-payer insurer approach, such positions enjoy little public support today, and governments of all ideological stripes have opted to work within the existing policy framework.

Education is a third sphere where public support for the public system—at both the K–12 and postsecondary levels—hasn't meaningfully wavered, despite left-right shifts in the political landscape. Nationwide, the proportion of school-age children enrolled in the public system ranges from 87.3 per cent in Quebec to 98.7 per cent in New Brunswick (in most provinces, the figure exceeds 90 per cent, when separate Roman Catholic schools are included).[10] Despite criticisms of the system, only a trickle of students leave the public system in favour of options such as private schools, charter schools and home schooling.

In the U.S., where the public school system has served as the stage for some of America's most fraught racial struggles, the nationwide figures are comparable, at first glance: 9.7 per cent of children were in the private system in 2013, a figure that had actually dropped from 11.2 per cent in 2003.[11] Four in five children enrolled in the private system are in religious schools (there's no constitutionally protected separate school system in the U.S.).[12] The proportion attending private schools also rises with income—more than a quarter of children living in families earning over $200,000 per year attend private schools—making the growing class-based segregation most apparent in classrooms.

The most significant difference between education policy in the two countries has to do with the funding of public schools. In Canada, since reforms adopted in all provinces during the mid- to late 1990s, provincial funding formulas have guaranteed that education dollars follow the students, regardless of where they live. In the U.S., by contrast, school boards are funded through the local, state and federal governments, but the lion's share comes from property taxes—a system that produces huge differences in school funding in wealthy and poor communities.

The system encourages middle- and upper-income families to abandon schools in lower-income areas, and it perpetuates (very often racialized) poverty because poor children end up attending underresourced schools.

One symptom of this disparity is the rapid growth of the charter school system, which now has over 2.5 million students in 6,500 academies. Charter schools don't charge tuition, and they operate independently from school boards and teachers' unions.[13] From 2003 to 2013, the proportion of children in public charter schools more than tripled, from 1.6 per cent to 5.1 per cent.[14] These institutions increasingly cater to families that have lost confidence in the public system, although they're more popular among Hispanic than black families, and their existence explicitly underscores the weaknesses of some school districts, especially in states like California, which has seen its property tax base and school budgets gutted by property tax revolts. The fact that the charter movement never caught on in Canada outside of Alberta suggests that most Canadian parents still patronize a public institution that plays a significant role in allowing newcomer families to establish and integrate themselves into the social mainstream.

The postsecondary education realm offers a similar picture. There are no private universities in Canada, which has enabled 44 per cent of newcomers to enroll in a college or university within four years of arriving.[15] In the U.S., which has many of the world's most prestigious research universities, the postsecondary story continues to be dogged by lower attendance among minority students and females, eye-popping tuition fees in the most elite schools and stubbornly high drop-out rates. "For the U.S. to maintain its global competitiveness," noted an evaluation by the

nonprofit Educational Testing Service in Princeton, New Jersey, "dramatic changes are needed to improve American post-secondary education."[16]

NONE OF THIS is to suggest that all Canadians are on the same page about their shared institutions and services. Ask an otherwise healthy retiree who's found himself on a seemingly interminable hip replacement waiting list, or a mother dealing with the leaden bureaucracy of the local school board, if they're sanguine about the state of health care and public education, and the answer is likely to be no.

Similarly, the high level of support among Canadians for ethnocultural diversity doesn't necessarily mean that some people won't look askance at new neighbours whose religious customs are unfamiliar, or cast votes for traditionalist politicians who hint at bringing in more socially conservative policies if elected. The question is whether shared public services offer a suitably weighty counterbalance to the socioeconomic and racial sorting that is redrawing the geographies of our largest urban regions. Does the taxi driver with the PhD who can't find suitable work become radicalized in his marginalization? Does his anger trigger a backlash among affluent urbanites, who lose confidence in immigration if low-income newcomers become more dependent on social services instead of becoming culturally integrated citizens contributing to the country's economic growth?

The answer is that there seems to be a constellation of other factors and shared values that have prevented this kind of downwards spiral—some combination of policies that do produce upwards mobility plus, crucially, a public discourse that emphasizes the benefits of a tolerant and welcoming society as opposed to a closed and hostile one.

In fact, the politics of economic resentment—which has fueled but doesn't entirely explain the rise of Trumpism—depends on a pathological form of polarization that has tended not to find much of an audience in those countries that, like Canada, consistently find themselves at the top of global happiness rankings.

CHAPTER SIX

Occupy This—The Politics of Inequality in Canada

The Occupy movement, which percolated to the top of public consciousness when income inequality protesters seized Zuccotti Park in lower Manhattan in 2011, never really had a coherent agenda. Philosophically, it was never meant to.

The anarchic protests and public space occupations spread organically all over the world, putting a face to the economic mayhem that ravaged so many countries after the 2008 credit crisis. The Occupiers evoked memories of the mass antiglobalization protests of the late 1990s and anticipated the confrontational civil disobedience of the Black Lives Matter movement that surged across North America in 2014 after a wave of police shootings of young black men in Ferguson, Baltimore, New York and many other places.

These three movements didn't really overlap and each had its own themes and drivers. But in some important ways, they all highlighted the way current power structures—global, national or local—exclude large segments of the population, sometimes forcibly and sometimes with lethal consequences.

After 2011, "the one percent" became instantly recognizable shorthand for those who sought to highlight the way the lion's share of a society's financial capital ends up in the hands of a relatively small number of rich people (although the more interesting statistic focuses on the wealth controlled by the top 0.01 per cent—the bankers and executives and business owners whose eight-figure incomes have achieved, as *The Atlantic* noted, "escape velocity" since the 1990s[1]). "The conflict between rich and poor," the *New York Times* opined in early 2012, "is now the greatest source of tension in American society."

The Occupy movement drew the attention of a small army of academics, analysts and pundits who had been warning—in academic journals and dry position papers—about the perils of growing wealth polarization and income inequality for years. Their ranks included the likes of Nobel Prize–winning economists Paul Krugman and Joseph Stiglitz, as well as the eminent British academic Richard Wilkinson, who spent a career explaining the "social epidemiology" of inequality and the myriad ways income polarization not only inflicts social costs but also exacts a psychological and physiological toll on those who find themselves in the bottom quintiles. In his doorstop treatise, *Capital*, the French economist Thomas Piketty served up hundreds of pages of quantitative proof that in capitalist economies the rich do, in fact, get richer.

The New Yorker's George Packer, author of *The Unwinding*, set out to document the lives of those stuck in the mire of a global economy that assigned more importance to cheap plastic products than stable unionized jobs. Matthew Desmond, an ethnographer, went to live with desperately poor families in Cincinnati's slums and trailer parks to investigate how eviction was playing a deeply corrosive role in low-income communities.[2] More recently, J. D. Vance, a San Francisco–based investment banker, added to the genre with *Hillbilly Elegy*, his memoir of growing up in a vio-

lence- and drug-filled white working-class household in an Ohio steel town.[3] On the other side of the racial divide, *The Atlantic*'s Ta-Nehisi Coates has powerfully documented the precariousness of black life in twenty-first-century America. His reporting has helped spur the renewed popularity of novelist James Baldwin, a trenchant critic of the black racism that has stained the entire history of the United States.

The outpouring of commentary and coverage about the Occupy movement clearly had an impact on public opinion in the U.S., but the story in Canada played out somewhat differently. In 2011, two-thirds of Canadians felt that the gap between rich and poor was widening. But that figure had dropped since 2008 and also marked a twenty-year low.[4] Canadians inclined to this view of the world overwhelmingly blame politics—tax breaks for corporations or the wealthy rather than the natural workings of global capitalism—but we also sense that inequality is worse in the United States.

About half of Canadians believe government still has a duty to implement strong policies to reduce inequality. Support for that outlook hasn't changed substantially since 2008, despite the change in government from minority Conservative to majority Conservative and, as of late 2015, majority Liberal. Those strongly opposed to public policies meant to fight inequality actually dropped from 12 per cent in 2008 to 6 per cent in 2017, a sign that most Canadians still believe in income redistribution to smooth out the inequities created by a market economy.

In 2014, only three in ten Americans felt that governments should tackle the issue—evidence, perhaps, that the urgency of the Occupy movement had faded. Yet the 2016 presidential marathon witnessed what seemed like a resurgence of public concern about inequality. Both Trump and Senator Bernie Sanders, the lone-wolf

Vermont Democratic Socialist, sought to exploit voter discontent about economic marginalization, Wall Street's influence and the outsourcing of jobs all in an effort to power their outsider campaigns against political insiders. While Trump's appeal was deeply rooted in all sorts of other resentments (especially race and sexism), Sanders offered up a populist program whose unabashed socialist policies—free college tuition, rejecting campaign contributions from "greedy" corporations—could have rivaled even the most stalwart Canadian New Democrat.

Sanders certainly carved out a space way to the left of NDP leader Thomas Mulcair, who, as leader of the official opposition, went into the 2015 federal election looking to secure an historic victory with a platform focused on, of all things, fiscal restraint. An NDP government, he assured voters, would balance the federal budget, not what most of us think of as classic socialism.

To those Canadians who craved a more activist vision of government and aligned their values around universal public services like health care, Mulcair's tack was not merely uninspiring; it represented a bewildering departure from the anti-elitist class resentment that's long formed the core of the NDP's outlook. After all, the NDP had been working the income inequality angle long before it became a politically carbonated cause in the wake of the 2011 Occupy movement. Way back in 1972, the social democratic saint David Lewis fought a federal election campaign on a platform attacking "corporate welfare bums."

Trudeau's Liberals—historically masters at the old trick of campaigning from the left and governing from the right—didn't miss the gift Mulcair presented to them. As the 2015 campaign reached its critical phase, Trudeau outflanked Mulcair, pledging to run a deficit and use infrastructure spending to prime the economic pump and spur job creation on important public works projects from coast to coast to coast. In effect, the Liberals and the NDP had swapped spots on the ideological spectrum.

Trudeau's Liberals bear scant resemblance to the legion of Sanders supporters. Millennial Americans felt the "Bern" more acutely than younger Canadians embraced Trudeau's "sunny ways." Where Sanders targeted voters who had been pushed to the side by trade, globalization and a tax system that allowed billionaire bosses to pay proportionally less tax than their clerical worker secretaries, the Liberals went after the urban middle classes, promising a tax cut, to be funded—with a nod to the passions stirred up by income inequality activists—by asking "the wealthiest one percent of Canadians to give a little more."[5] The positioning obviously found its mark, although the Liberals could never be accused of playing to the sort of populist passions that Sanders ignited with his insurgent run to prevent Hillary Clinton's coronation.

THESE CONTRASTS, AS well as the NDP's unsuccessful drift towards the political centre, raise an interesting question: How does the politics of income inequality play out in Canada in 2017, if at all?

First, the high-level context. In both Canada and the U.S., the post–World War II decades—with their economic prosperity, abundance of unionized manufacturing jobs and high marginal tax rates where high earners pay proportionally more than those earning lower incomes—were marked by relatively little inequality, especially compared to the era of the robber barons and extremes of wealth and poverty during the Gilded Age in the late nineteenth century.

But income inequality has risen in Canada in the past few years after a period of relative stability that extended through much of the 2000s and early 2010s. According to the Conference Board of Canada, our "Gini coefficient," an internationally recognized measure of inequality for after-tax income (0 represents absolute equality; 1 denotes maximum inequality), has hovered at 0.32 for more than fifteen years. From the mid-1970s to the early 1990s, Canada's Gini score was lower—about 0.29—but inequality rose dramatically as Prime Minister Jean Chrétien's Liberal government slashed social transfers in order to reduce a severe deficit overhang. Canada's Gini then stabilized during the 2000s due to policies such as the Child Tax Benefit, which boosted household earnings in lower-income families and drastically reduced their net taxes.

For all its political salience, income inequality remains a slippery economic concept that becomes a potent social force only when the differences between classes become glaringly obvious—ostentatious mansions, prestige automobiles, outrageously expensive lifestyles and seemingly gratuitous status symbols publicly displayed by the superrich even as ordinary working people are thrown out of their jobs and visible homelessness proliferates.

Beyond the familiar symbols, overall measures of inequality grow when the incomes of one group rise faster than those of another group. As Statistics Canada economist Andrew Heisz has explained, it's possible to live in a period of growing inequality even if all wealth classes are experiencing rising income. That's what happened during the 2000s: everyone's earnings grew and inequality didn't change much. Between 2000 and 2011, in fact, the household earnings of the lowest quintile grew faster—24.3 per cent, in constant dollars—than either the middle or highest quintile.

Still, the top two quintiles, or the 40 per cent of Canadians with the highest after-tax market earnings, soaked up almost two-thirds of the country's income in 2010. The bottom two quintiles brought home just 20 per cent of the national income, or half of the 40 per

how individuals' circumstances can change over time. A society that tolerates a high degree of inequality and also provides little opportunity for people on the lower rungs to improve their lot is clearly doing worse than a society that somehow facilitates advancement through accessible public education, flexible labour markets, greater union membership, an abundance of mixed-income neighbourhoods, or perhaps even a proliferation of porous social networks and, dare I say, less systemic racism.

For many generations, U.S. political and business leaders have advocated the rags-to-riches Horatio Alger/American dream mythology, which holds that anyone, no matter how poor or disadvantaged, can bootstrap his or her way up the greasy pole thanks to a combination of hard work, entrepreneurship and a positive mind-set.

Liberal Canadians tend to pooh-pooh the American dream as delusional thinking, yet most nevertheless subscribe to the ideas underneath the Hollywood rhetoric. According to University of Ottawa economist Miles Corak—whose 2010 Pew study, *Chasing the Same Dream, Climbing Different Ladders*, compares economic mobility in the U.S. and Canada—people on both sides of the 49th parallel share many deeply held beliefs about the nature of social and economic advancement and equality of opportunity.

Even in the shadow of a devastating downturn, Americans generally were more likely than Canadians to believe their children would be better off than they were. Americans were also less inclined than Canadians (42 per cent compared to 57 per cent) to agree that someone's financial success was related to a parent's wealth. Finally, Corak's surveys found that Americans—again, not surprisingly—were more likely than Canadians to view government as an impediment to individual advancement.

But then a funny thing happened on the way to the country club. Corak's analysis, which has been replicated subsequently, found that in the U.S., the confines of class, that dreaded British notion, are actually much more rigid than many Americans are prepared to admit. What's more, Canadians seem to enjoy more upward mobility—doing better in terms of income than their parents—despite the fact that our governments tend to be more interventionist when it comes to markets. Corak found that the children of top-earning Americans were more likely than their Canadian counterparts to earn top incomes. At the other end of the spectrum, the children of poor Americans were more likely to remain poor compared to their Canadian equivalents (38 per cent to 30 per cent).

A recent Stanford University study by economist Raj Chetty puts this story into an even more international context. "In the United States," he observes, "children born to parents in the bottom fifth of the income distribution have a 7.5 percent chance of reaching the top fifth. That compares with about 9.0 percent in the United Kingdom, 11.7 percent in Denmark, and 13.5 percent in Canada." Indeed, when the media picked up those results, some headline writers gleefully pointed out that the best way to achieve the American dream was to become a Canadian. The figures, as Chetty explains, indicate that a Canadian child born to poor parents is twice as likely to "make it" compared to that American youngster who may be living in a social housing complex or a trailer park or a rural community that's seen its industrial base collapse.[8]

None of this is to say there isn't entrenched, intergenerational poverty in Canada, of a sort that is every bit as all-encompassing and bleak as what you'd find in a depressed coal-mining town in West Virginia or a crime-ridden housing project in East Los Angeles. The suicide rates of Indigenous youth living in very isolated communities or the grinding poverty that confronts addicts living on the streets of Vancouver's Downtown Eastside attest to the fact that Canada's social safety net has plenty of holes and that pathways to middle-class success can be highly elusive for systemically marginalized Canadians.

But in the aggregate, Canada's economic mobility story reveals a great deal about why perceptions of inequality are tempered by other experiences.

Further evidence of this can be found in the UN's World Happiness Report, which combines nation-level surveys of life satisfaction with measures of quantitative factors—such as GDP per capita and life expectancy—and qualitative ones such as trust and generosity. Since the United Nations began systematically measuring national mood five years ago, Canada has consistently been in the top ten, along with those same Scandinavians who are so famous for organizing their societies around egalitarian ideals. In fact, on the 2017 World Happiness ranking, we managed to edge out Sweden.

As data gathered by the left-leaning Washington-based Institute for Policy Studies shows, the countries with higher happiness scores are more egalitarian in terms of the distribution of incomes. Interestingly, the top 1 per cent's income share is approximately the same for Canada, the U.K. and Germany—about 13 per cent in 2015—and yet Canadians are happier than the citizens of either of the other two nations, according to those same metrics. The U.S., as in all these statistics, remains an outlier: plenty of wealth and income inequality, not very happy.

The degree of inequality in Canada is held in check by other features of the economy, such as unionization. It's true that far fewer people belong to unions today than during the postwar period and up to the early 1980s, when more than four in ten Canadians were members of labour organizations that negotiated better wages, improved working conditions and defined benefits pension plans.

That proportion plunged after Canada signed the Free Trade Agreement (and subsequently its contentious successor, the North American Free Trade Agreement). But the decline in labour representation leveled out in the early 2000s. Today, public sector unions and some of the legacy private sector unions still employ about 26 per cent of the Canadian labour force,[9] which is well below the rates in the Scandinavian nations but nonetheless significantly above the OECD average (17 per cent). And despite the deep economic integration between Canada and the U.S., our union membership is well above that of our southern neighbour, where less than 11 per cent of the workforce belongs to a union.[10]

Health measures offer another way of illustrating the relationship between inequality and other social issues. In the U.S., many important health indicators have been trending in the wrong direction: obesity,[11] death rates for black children[12] and the incidence of chronic conditions like diabetes (while diabetes rates in 2014 were seven times higher than they were in the late 1950s, the growth has tailed off slightly in the past few years).[13] A March 2017 *Washington Post* investigation found that the number of people receiving long-term disability payments in rural and predominantly white counties facing a decline in employment has increased by as much as 64 per cent since 2004 (the rates were far higher than in big cities like Washington, D.C.).[14] Moreover, life expectancy is actually declining, startling given the amount of money Americans spend on health care—U.S. per capita health spending is double that of most other OECD nations. "This is a big deal," said Philip Morgan, a demographer at the University of North Carolina at

Chapel Hill. "There's not a better indicator of well-being than life expectancy."[15]

Canadian life expectancy figures have been moving in the other direction, with males predicted to see the greatest gains in longevity in coming decades. A 2017 study by *The Lancet* predicted that Canadian men born between 2010 and 2030, along with their counterparts in Australia and New Zealand, can expect to live the longest lives of all the nations surveyed.

A related indicator, and one that may play a role in the growing gap between rich and poor, is the financial burden that health-care expenses place on individuals and families.

In Canada, there's little public appetite for dismantling the single-payer health-care system, which is built around provincial spending and federal transfers, bulk purchasing of pharmaceuticals by provincial formulary, pharmacare for seniors, private health insurance provided by employers, philanthropic donations to health-care facilities, federal research funding and partially subsidized long-term care. Court decisions in the 2000s have allowed individuals to purchase private care, but these clinics serve only a tiny slice of the population.

Canadians, however, increasingly find themselves forced to pay huge sums for drug treatments, and these financial burdens can be ruinous, especially for those with rare conditions. Moreover, with the advent of highly specialized drug therapies, the price of treatment can be extravagant and may not be covered by insurance.

Stories about families facing crushing drug bills get lots of media attention, but how prevalent is the problem? A 2014 U.S. National Institutes of Health examination of five thousand representative personal bankruptcy cases in Canada found that almost

half of the respondents faced some loss of income because of illness or care-giving responsibilities. Sixty per cent also reported
that they'd had to pay a medical bill, but only a tiny fraction faced
one exceeding $5,000.[16]

The narrative south of the border is far different. The *American
Journal of Medicine* points out that in 1981, only 6 per cent of
families declaring bankruptcy cited medical reasons; by 2009, the
proportion had shot up to 62.1 per cent—equivalent to more than
600,000 cases per month. Subsequent evaluations of the drivers
of medical bankruptcies showed that even those with employer-
provided health insurance end up bankrupt as the cost of treatment
exceeds the caps on their insurance policies.

These figures are not without controversy. The Fraser Institute,
using mid-2000s data, contended that Canada's reported medical
bankruptcy numbers aren't significantly lower than America's.
And Snopes, a fact-checking site, cites other academic research
that concluded that medical bankruptcy accounts for less than a
quarter of U.S. insolvencies. The picture is further muddied by the
fact that some families declare bankruptcy because of job problems exacerbated by medical bills.[17]

The deep contentiousness around health care in the U.S.—not
just the political fate of the Affordable Care Act (Obamacare) but
also the overall cost of the system and the spiraling financial burdens of health-related policies, such as the federal government's
$192-billion-a-year disability benefits program—underscores the
fact that almost all other affluent nations have chosen not to rel-
egate these sets of services to the vagaries of the market and the
employment status of individuals.

Unsurprisingly, the strains associated with health care affect
stress levels. The American Psychological Association regularly

conducts large-scale surveys of stress levels in the U.S. Stress—
about work, money, family and health—tends to rise and fall in
sync with the economy's performance. In recent years, the picture
has improved, although a February 2017 APA survey found that
stress levels spiked after Trump's election.[18] Despite the general
reduction in stress levels, 72 per cent of Americans reported feeling anxious about money, and for a good chunk of those, the concern was health care. "Nearly one in five Americans say that they
have either considered skipping or skipped going to the doctor in
the past year when they needed health care because of financial
concerns," the APA concluded. And that's *despite* the fact that
Obamacare brought coverage to twenty million previously unin-
sured Americans.

Estimates of Canadians' stress levels vary, but StatCan's Community Health Survey offers a revealing comparison. Using data
gathered from 2003 to 2013, the results show that while Canadian
women tend to report more stress than men, there's been little net
change over a decade in the proportion of people over fifteen who
say they are a bit or extremely stressed—the figure hovers around
23–25 per cent of the population. Those numbers don't fluctuate
sharply with the state of the economy. They dropped very gradu-
ally as the economy improved during the early to mid-2000s, then
trended up somewhat after the 2009 recession before leveling off to
the rate that existed in 2003.[19]

This picture reveals some important realities. Thanks to strict
regulatory oversight, Canada's banks didn't crater during the financial crisis. Nor were there neighbourhoods where the combination of plunging property values and skyrocketing subprime
mortgages left many homeowners "underwater," with the market
value of their homes dipping below the amount owing on their

loans. Medical bankruptcies didn't become big news; indeed, health-care spending in Canada for much of the past decade has grown faster than inflation, and the principal concern about access to care focused more on finding a family doctor or quickly locating a specialist for elective surgery than losing a life's savings to medical or pharmaceutical bills.

THE BROADER POINT about these cross-border comparisons is that the degree of income inequality is related in complex and circular ways to a host of other issues.

While it is well known that rates of violent crime, homicide and incarceration are much higher in the United States than in Canada, sometimes by a factor of six or seven to one, what is less well known is the number of people walking around with criminal records. A criminal record affects someone for the rest of his or her life, for example, the ability to vote (in many states in the U.S., but not in Canada, where even prisoners can vote) and securing employment and credit (a problem in both countries). Public Safety Canada (which is responsible for the RCMP and federal penitentiaries) reports that in 2009, 3.8 million Canadians had criminal records. This was about 11 per cent of our population.

In the U.S., a report by the Bureau of Justice Statistics using state-by-state records reports that the roughly equivalent proportion in 2012 was about 30 per cent, with fairly substantial state-to-state variation. As with incarceration, the proportions of African-Americans with criminal records is much higher in the U.S., and in Canada Indigenous peoples are more likely to have similar status. And of course men are more likely than women to commit crimes. Simple drug possession convictions feature largely in that alarming statistic. Can you imagine a country in which nearly one-third of the population has a criminal record, and all the lingering social and economic disadvantages that stain inflicts?

Such social crises create a vicious, downwards spiral: the stress of not having enough money or being excluded from the workforce because of a criminal record is exacerbated by unexpected medical bills, which may trigger illness and disability that result in a loss of income, more strain, more illness and more difficulty for other family members.

In their 2009 bestseller, *The Spirit Level: Why Equality Is Better for Everyone*, the British epidemiologists Richard Wilkinson and Kate Pickett point out that more inequality is correlated with a lengthy list of social problems, including less trust, mental illness, low life expectancy, obesity, educational performance of young children, teenage birth rates, the incidence of homicide and imprisonment rates. Overall gains in GDP, a standard proxy for a country's economic well-being, don't reduce the social distances between people, and the resulting stratification becomes a breeding ground for resignation, resentment and anger.

Drawing on extensive standardized data from OECD nations as well as individual U.S. states, Wilkinson and Pickett unpacked the insidious impact of inequality and showed how this kind of income polarization is strongly correlated to high infant mortality, premature death, chronic illness and addiction. Echoing the APA's findings, they also showed how the ambient stress of highly unequal societies—"increased inequality ups the stakes in the competition for status"—worms its way "under [the] skin" of those at the bottom or middle of the ladder. Chronic stress is closely associated with a range of physical ailments: cardiovascular illness, stroke, diabetes. Some researchers, in fact, have shown that permanently elevated cortisol levels in pregnant women can be transmitted to their fetuses, adding an intergenerational physiological response to inequality-based stress.

This is classic sociology. As humans evolve due to improving economies and technological progress, switching from day-to-day survival to personal fulfillment, we move on from absolute deprivation to relative deprivation. Once we are able to enjoy the basics of food, clothing and shelter, our "needs" become more "positional." We look for our place in the status hierarchy. We compare ourselves to our peers—first our siblings, then our friends and finally those in our community.

If others are doing a lot better than we are, we could rationalize our lower position by concluding that we are not smart enough or not diligent enough. Alternatively, we might attribute our situation to disadvantage (our gender, race, ethnicity, social class, disability). In the U.S., the official founding ideology says success is a proof of virtue (the Puritan ethic) while failure is evidence of the absence of virtue. In Canada, by contrast, we see the merits of both arguments: yes we should defer gratification, do our homework and pull up our own socks. But we also acknowledge that not everyone was born on third base with the advantages good luck and our parents gave us. For that reason, we see a role for government to level the playing field a bit so poor kids can grow up to be good parents, which allows them and their children to have happy, fulfilling lives.[20]

On almost all the measures Wilkinson and Pickett include in *The Spirit Level*, Canada, which ranks in the middle of OECD nations in terms of its inequality, also tends to fall in the middle of the pack with most indicators, either slightly above or below the median.

Their data, of course, reflects what was going on in the 2000s. In the past few years, inequality in Canada has edged up, but other elements of the picture—mobility, education scores, health, happiness—suggest that something else has been happening as well. Some observers have identified what they regard as signs of a troubling decline, including more alienated voters and basement-dwelling millennials consigned to the shadows of the gig economy.

But successive surveys, both domestic and international, have shown that a large majority of Canadians are either very or somewhat satisfied with their standard of living, comfortable with the extent of the country's cultural, sexual and ethnic diversity and engaged with the world. Between 2010 and 2017, the number of Canadians who described their economic situation as good increased from 38 per cent to 52 per cent, while those who said they weren't doing well dropped from 20 per cent to 14 per cent.

Indeed, the discontents of inequality and its myriad social symptoms have failed to stir Canadians politically, and this fact helps to explain the absence of a welling up of the sort of angry populist, anti-immigrant sentiment that has taken root in the U.S., France and the U.K.

As Environics's 2016 survey on the state of the country's governance concluded, most Canadians believe the federal government is generally working, rather than broken, and confidence has actually grown since the 2015 election. It's not that we're in love with everything our decision makers do—we're not. Yet our resentments tend to be more regional in nature, and they mainly yield to our boring instinct for compromise over confrontation. Overall, the evidence nationally shows that Canadians and their governments have managed, over a period of decades, to prevent or mitigate the accumulation of corrosive social forces that finally surfaced angrily in the populist politics of the Trump/Brexit era.

CHAPTER SEVEN

Doing Democracy Differently?

As grassroots movements go, the one that sparked to life during Toronto's dull 2006 municipal race showed the kind of staying power most activists only dream about. That year, a group of young people held a series of "auditions" for candidates for city council. The process was open and lively, and it produced a slate of fresh faces in an election that featured, as is often the case, the predictable coronations of veteran councillors who get re-elected because people recognize their names or happen to have one of their magnets on the fridge.

None of these energetic reformers got elected, but a few, including Dave Meslin, decided to continue the fight to improve politics by making it more inclusive.

Over the next several years, Meslin built a coalition of electoral reformers who would coalesce into a movement that sought to replace the traditional "first-past-the-post" system of determining winners with a so-called ranked-ballots approach that allowed voters to preselect second, third or fourth choices. In this automated system, there would be successive ballots. Each round, the least popular candidates would be dropped until one of the remaining competitors marshaled over 50 per cent of the votes. Variations of the system are used to choose leaders for Canadian political parties, and the ranked-ballots technique is also employed in a number of jurisdictions around the world.

According to Meslin and other election reform activists, the change in the voting system would crack the spine of incumbency at the municipal level and provide an entry for more diverse candidates. It would also produce sturdier outcomes in parliamentary elections, which in recent decades have featured winners who garner less than half the popular vote after campaigns in which turnout barely noses above 60 per cent (or even lower, as in municipal races)—in other words, governments elected by a minority of a bare majority.

Meslin's ranked-ballots warriors, who saw themselves as progressive populists, pushed and wheedled and publicized, eventually securing first a commitment from Toronto council, then legislation from Kathleen Wynne's government, and finally a pledge from Justin Trudeau's Liberals to overhaul the federal voting system so 2015 would be the last ever first-past-the-post election.

They were ecstatic, but then something curious happened. First, the Toronto council reversed its position and voted not to adopt ranked-ballots elections, even after the provincial government had passed a law allowing them. Then, amidst the mayhem of Donald Trump's first days in office, the Trudeau Liberals pulled the plug on all talk of voting reform, ending a ponderous (and botched) consultation process that sought Canadians' views on the state of a core democratic institution. After a few days of predictable flaying in the press, the issue of voting reform disappeared beneath the waves—an entirely predictable outcome, given the complexity of the proposed reform and the absence of a groundswell of public outrage.

. . . .

THESE FLIP-FLOPS RAISE uncomfortable questions: Are the Trudeau Liberals saying they've studied the issues and determined that all's well—nothing to look at here? Or does the fact that they broke a core election pledge serve as a reminder that Canadian democracy has always been a game played by and for elites? Is the political class circling the wagons?

In an age of roiling populist politics that has seen the emergence of ultranationalists and authoritarians, the Liberals' gestures— both the promise and then the abandonment of reform—may seem like so much tinkering at the edges of a system that hasn't changed much since Pierre Trudeau repatriated the constitution in 1982.

But if we're trying to figure out whether an anti-immigrant/ nationalist strain of populism could take root here in a serious way, we need to look closely at the sturdiness of our own parliamentary institutions. We should also scrutinize the structural weaknesses that may have allowed other democracies to slide away from core principles (human rights, rule of law) or make impulsive choices that will almost certainly foster economic instability or increase vulnerability to violence.

In the case of Brexit, for example, the result didn't merely reflect a swing in public opinion towards an isolationist, anti-immigrant agenda. Younger Britons, who overwhelmingly backed Remain, were justifiably outraged that they'd have to live for decades with the fallout of what will inevitably be an immensely costly decision backed by older voters, most of whom won't. In the aftermath, journalists dug up legions of Leave supporters who publicly admitted that they regretted their choices. Some of the leading political spokespersons for the Leave side also abandoned the cause, while

Farage stepped down as party leader, effectively signaling that he'd accomplished his mission. Last, the referendum, which had been advocated by former prime minister David Cameron, went ahead, even though voters had no idea how much the whole thing would cost (preliminary estimates, made public after Prime Minister Theresa May formally initiated the exit process in early 2017, make it clear the bill will be crushing). Yes, there should be ways for ordinary voters to defy elites; at the same time, there's clearly something wrong with this picture. Britons don't look like a society satisfied with their deliberative process and ready to enjoy the fruits of this exercise of direct democracy.

As for the U.S., Trump's election marked the second time in a generation where the candidate with fewer popular votes won the election—a stunning indictment of the antiquated electoral college system. But as many traditional conservative commentators have acknowledged, Trump's ascendancy underscored not just the failings of the epic nomination process but also the extreme and worsening polarization that has beset American politics and its democratic institutions.

While all democracies depend on partisan competition to frame debates about crucial matters of public interest, it's difficult to conclude that all's well in a system marked by hyper-partisanship, entrenched stand-offs, the corrupting influence of dark money and the conspicuous absence of any kind of compromise dynamic (once upon a time, the Senate's role was to reconcile the factionalism of the House, but those days seem to be well and truly over). None of this started with Trump, nor are the Republicans the only ones to blame. But when a staunch conservative pundit like Canadian-born David Frum, a former George W. Bush speechwriter, sounds a dire warning about how a Trump-led government could descend into an autocracy with fascistic undertones, it's not difficult to conclude that something's gone wrong with the democratic institutions that produce so much gridlock.

The nineteenth-century American historian Henry Adams (descendant of two presidents but no relation to me) famously observed that "politics, as a practice . . . has always been the systematic organization of hatreds." It's a great line and still true. But when the most visible sworn defender of the U.S. Constitution attacks no less than the First Amendment by vilifying the media as "enemies of the people," you know the problems run deeper than politics as usual.

IT'S POSSIBLE, OF course, that the pan-national surge of anti-immigrant populism reflects the reality that human beings aren't all that good at managing tolerance, rapid change and fear. When the watering hole shrinks, as the old saying goes, the animals look at each other differently. The liberalism of mid-nineteenth-century Europe gave way to the violence and totalitarianism of the early twentieth century. The idealism of the 1960s gave way to the culture wars and retrenchment of the 1970s and 1980s. These grand currents are about much more than the fine points of voting, the wording of referendum questions or how judges get appointed.

There's some evidence that we've arrived at one of those historical junctures. Roberto Stefan Foa, a University of Melbourne political scientist, and Yascha Mounk, a lecturer on government at Harvard, have compiled jarring evidence of a clear generational skew on the subject of whether democracy is essential. In their widely discussed essay, "The Signs of Deconsolidation," they cited data from Australia, the U.K., the U.S., Netherlands, New Zealand and Sweden, showing that young people in most of these nations were far less invested in democracy than their elders.[1] With the exception of Sweden, only 30 per cent to 40 per cent of people in their thirties in the other five countries felt democracy is "essential." That figure rises to the 70–80 per cent range for seniors. (In Sweden, 60 per cent of young people say democracy is essential.)[2]

These trends are apparent in Canada. While about three-quarters of those aged sixty-five to seventy-four voted in the 2011 federal election, the turnout rate for the eighteen-to-twenty-four cohort was just 40 per cent. Elections Canada says this pattern has been evident in every election since 2004, the year it started performing generational comparisons.

If this dynamic continues, the decline of voting in the twenty-first century may become as striking a phenomenon as the fall-off in church attendance in the late 1950s and 1960s. Baby boomers left the church; their children and grandchildren seem to be drifting away from the state.

One reason for declining turnout is a deep shift in social values away from deference to institutional authority. It used to be that if society's leaders told us to do something, we did as we were told. Now people are more likely to make personal calculations about whether voting is worth the effort. Canadians are also less driven by a sense of duty than they once were. Eighty-three per cent of Canadians over sixty say voting is a duty; 48 per cent of those eighteen to thirty-nine agree. Foa and Mounk's research also reveals how some millennials are more inclined to accept authoritarian rule.

Almost three decades after the fall of communism, the allure of the strong leader seems to be on the upswing around the world.

Former Soviet Bloc countries like Hungary and Poland are weakening their democracies. Turkey, though never a paragon of democracy, has found itself hurtling towards authoritarian rule as President Recep Tayyip Erdoğan won a referendum that permits a significant degradation in democratic checks and balances. While opposition critics and independent observers warned about electoral irregularities, Donald Trump, tellingly, was one of the first Western leaders to call Erdoğan to congratulate him for, in effect, eroding the political rights of his citizens.

Many factors have driven these structural changes. After the chaos and loss of status that marked Boris Yeltsin's tenure during the botched liberalization of the early post-Soviet era, Putin made it his mission to, well, make Russia great again, and if that meant murdering journalists and invading a neighbour as a warning shot, so be it. In much of Europe and the U.S., fear of terrorism (exacerbated by huge refugee flows) has produced a large constituency for tough-talking politicians who aren't afraid to trample rights and drop bombs. In Europe, as well, the years of economic stagnation that followed the 2008 financial crisis have prompted people in many countries, not just the U.K., to lose faith in the euro, the animating ideals of the European Union and its bureaucratically cumbersome institutions.[3]

In fact, the rise of anti-immigrant populism in the EU is, in some ways, a rejection of all the liberal, postnational ideas that formed the foundation of the Eurozone. The Eurocrats in Brussels couldn't, in the end, offer a satisfactory solution to earthquake-like problems such as the implosion of the Greek economy or the refugee crisis in Syria and elsewhere. The structural downplaying of ethnic identity, coupled with the EU's leap of faith about how trade and labour market liberalization would lift all the boats, were intellectual constructs of Europe's elites (i.e., Germany). As it turns out, those ideas have proved to be highly vulnerable to the old prejudices and national resentments that still fester in the shadows of European society. In fact, some people, especially immigrants packed into the monolithic high rises and suburban tracts ringing many European cities, didn't even have a boat.

As in Europe, the ascendancy of American far-right populism is also grounded in smoldering hatreds that coalesced around a group of political renegades—first the Tea Party, then Trump—who created safe spaces (Fox, Breitbart, Infowars) for the airing of all those "politically incorrect" views.

But these forces also draw their strength from relatively recent changes to the creaky machinery of American democracy, with its built-in mechanisms for distributing authority widely. Anyone who's sat through an American history class knows that the eighteenth-century founders sought a balance of power designed to handcuff would-be autocrats; they'd had enough of kings. The three branches—judicial, executive and legislative—are constitutionally compelled to share governance, not just with one another but also with the states and individuals.

From the get-go, it was an inherently conservative system designed to move slowly and recognize new rights—like those that blacks, women, gays, lesbians and trans people would eventually seek—grudgingly. Due to the deeply fractured nature of American political culture, some hot-button topics (gun control, abortion, voting rights, privacy) have either become or simply remained profoundly contested issues that sharply define the contours of public opinion from election to election, and generation to generation.

But several other critical factors have served to accelerate and entrench the polarization that afflicts American politics. Some are older; others more recent.

Until President Lyndon Johnson signed the Voting Rights Act of 1965, many jurisdictions, especially in the South, found both overt and coercive ways of preventing black Americans from registering to vote. The new law allowed the federal Justice Department to oversee counties with long histories of voter suppression. But the 2013 Supreme Court ruling in *Shelby County v. Holder* gutted those provisions and ushered in a new era of more subtle voter suppression as numerous states rushed to pass laws requiring residents to jump through bureaucratic hoops in order to register.[4] The laws, reminiscent of the way county clerks in the South required blacks to pass Jim Crow literacy tests in order to register, effectively exclude nonwhite voters, especially in rural and lower-income communities—a situation that favours conservative white voters who back policies such as aggressively enforced deportation laws. The race to enact these new laws didn't stop Trump and many Republicans from raising the spectre of widespread voter fraud, despite the complete absence of reliable evidence confirming such alleged activity.

It's possible that when the U.S. becomes a minority-majority nation (2040s), these laws will either have been repealed or become completely redundant. But the fact that extreme partisanship still infects the laws governing the administration of American democracy imposes an additional type of partisan friction on politics. Elections are not just a competition of ideas about laws, spending and the administration of public institutions; they become contests about which lives count, which voices deserve a hearing, who's American enough to cast a ballot. No one should be surprised to discover that anti-immigrant populism can easily take root amidst such conflicts. As the author of one prepresidential election survey found, the single most reliable predictor of a Republican voter was the respondent's answer to the question, "Is Barack Obama a Muslim?" Fully 89 per cent of those who said yes were Trump supporters.

Since the early nineteenth century, American politicians have sought to draw electoral districts in order to gain partisan advantage (the word "gerrymander" was coined after Elbridge Gerry, governor of Massachusetts, approved oddly shaped districts). And while courts have ruled on several occasions that the practice itself is unconstitutional, they've refused to rule, as recently as 2004, on what precisely constitutes a gerrymander.

During the civil rights era, liberals endorsed a certain type of gerrymandering that was intended to create electoral districts with a sufficient concentration of minority voters that these communities could elect black or Hispanic candidates to the U.S. Congress or some state legislatures.

But political operatives learned how to game the system by using two approaches: "packing" and "cracking." With packing, the goal is to draw district boundaries that maximize the number of opposition voters in a single district. With cracking, the idea is to draw boundaries that carve up known voting blocs and thus dilute their electoral clout. In either case, the results are peculiarly shaped, meandering electoral districts that pay little attention to natural boundaries (highways, rivers, etc.).

In 2011, when the results of the 2010 census were about to be released, Republican operatives realized that they were standing, as *The New Yorker*'s Elizabeth Kolbert observed, in the path of "a looming demographic disaster." The party's brass stepped up an effort, dubbed REDMAP, to use tactical redistricting to eliminate Democratic seats in both the state legislatures and the U.S. Congress. When the dust settled, state-level Republicans had gained seven hundred districts across the U.S., and secured control of both houses in twenty-five legislatures. Among the states successfully targeted by the GOP's gerrymanders were Michigan and Pennsylvania, two of the so-called firewall states that delivered Trump's electoral college victory.[5]

Politicians everywhere will try to alter the rules of the game to maximize their own advantage in elections. But as with the fights over voter registration, the heightened attention to gerrymandering as a means of delivering victories reveals a system consumed by a sort of hyper-partisanship that tends to devalue policy debates. Such redistricting exercises also amplify the impact of growing social segregation. After all, as neighbourhoods become more homogeneous, this kind of gerrymandering guarantees that voters will be less likely to consider interests other than the ones that animate their own tribe—an energizing force that feeds into a form of politics that thrives on stigmatizing immigrants or minorities.

Money has also played a significant role in American democracy for many years, but the floodgates opened after the *Citizens United* Supreme Court ruling in 2010. Under the judgment, corporations and unions can now make unlimited campaign contributions. They may not contribute directly to a candidate, but instead direct their cash to so-called Super PACs, which spend those funds to promote a specific candidate, party or issue. The Citizens United decision paved the way for a form of anonymous financial influence by moneyed interests that has drastically reshaped the dynamic of subsequent elections, including the 2016 presidential race. Unlike conventional election fund-raising, there are no disclosure rules or spending limits because the Court ruled that private corporations have the same free speech rights as individuals.

These changes rapidly gathered momentum and resulted in a sharp increase in political spending by the superrich in the run-up to the 2016 election. Among those who backed Trump through a Super PAC was the reclusive hedge fund billionaire Robert Mercer, who is also a major investor in Breitbart, the white nationalist news site that Steve Bannon managed until he joined the Trump campaign.

The result is a vast and opaque system of campaign financing that relies on anonymity and attack ads (which are tactically deployed to reduce turnout), and produces a web of quid-pro-quo understandings between shadowy funders and the politicians they have purchased. (Attack ads predate *Citizens United*, but the ruling sharply increased the volume of such advertising.)

Every society's political institutions mirror, to some extent, the underlying (and at times contradictory) values of the members of that society. Americans, of course, zealously defend and uphold the right of individual citizens to oversee government institutions, which is why so many public officeholders—including judges, district attorneys, senior municipal administrators, as well as more nationally visible figures—are elected rather than appointed.

Yet the populism (and, some would say, anti-elitism) that's hard-wired into this far-flung system of democratic accountability constantly butts up against an equally potent impulse. Certain public figures—big-city mayors, governors, U.S. senators, the president—wield extensive powers, including the ability to hold office for decades, declare war unilaterally, and even make life and death decisions in capital crimes appeals. Indeed, the parade of sordid revelations about whether Trump had sought to suppress the FBI's investigations into Russian interference in the 2016 election revealed just how much power a president possesses: it's not just the nuclear codes.

Yet in a fractious country where almost half the population believes in the importance of authoritarian leadership and the level of religious observance considerably exceeds that of other advanced nations, it's hardly surprising to see the ascendancy of polarizing, populist politics.

American democracy—born of revolution and then severely tested in a civil war that sometimes seems strangely unresolved—has evolved to deliver just such an outcome.

HOW DOES CANADA measure up, with a democracy that is the product of generations of negotiated accommodations and grudging compromises among the ruling elites who have long had a tendency to view the masses with condescension? When it comes to voter turnout, Canada, like the U.S. and most other postindustrial nations, has seen a long-term decline in participation.[6] Low voter turnouts have become particularly pronounced among millennials and those who choose to express their political views by engaging with advocacy organizations or NGOs instead of political parties and voting.

Canada's turnout rate, according to Pew Research in a multi-country comparison, sat at 62 per cent of the eligible population for 2015 and 68 per cent of registered voters. That puts Canada ahead of the U.S., where just over half of eligible citizens vote, but it's in the middle of the pack for OECD nations. Turnout among registered voters in the U.S. is much higher (84 per cent), and the gap—the largest among all the countries surveyed by Pew except Luxemburg—reflects the fact that registering in the U.S. is not automatic, as it is in Canada and many other countries. Consequently, the political conflict around registration, rooted as it is in white Southerners' fear of black majorities in the post–Civil War South, is almost nonexistent here.

Things might have been different. In 2014, the Harper government introduced the Fair Elections Act, a sweeping voting reform law that made a number of key changes, two of which would have directly impacted turnout. One was putting an end to "vouching," i.e., allowing someone who didn't receive a voter registration card in the mail or preregister to sign up and vote at a local polling station on Election Day. The other sought to place strict limits on Elections Canada's efforts to drive up voter participation by promoting elections.

Both measures received intense criticism. *The Globe and Mail* ran a week-long series of editorials minutely dissecting the bill's failings. The Tories couldn't support their claim that vouching led to voter fraud. Nor was there a public policy case for not encouraging voters to exercise their franchise. Some observers saw an ulterior motive: by downplaying electoral participation in campaigns that feature more and more attack ads, the well-funded Conservatives were in a better position to mobilize their own base. The chief electoral officer, Jean-Pierre Kingsley, condemned the measures for discouraging participation. In the end, the Conservatives capitulated on the most contentious provisions. (Ironically, one of the few people convicted of election fraud in Canada was a Conservative organizer who spread misinformation about voting stations, known as voter suppression.)

In general, there is nothing comparable to the bitter political fights over alleged voter fraud that marred the 2016 U.S. election—battles that invariably call into question, however incorrectly, the integrity of the electoral process and serve to discourage participation.

The story of political fund-raising in Canada also reveals diverging paths. When Stephen Harper came to power in 2006, he was capitalizing on public indignation about the sponsorship scandal that occurred while Jean Chrétien's Liberals were in power. The scandal involved the cycling of cash from well-connected Quebec advertising firms through public "sponsorship" opportunities—basically, venues for promoting federal services to Quebec residents as a means of reminding them about Ottawa's role—with some of the funds recycled into party coffers. While Chrétien dismissed the allegations, Paul Martin, in an inadvertent act of political self-immolation, appointed an inquiry to examine the accusations. Harper successfully capitalized on the damaging revelations that surfaced during the hearings.

While the sponsorship scandal shone a damning spotlight on the role of grey money in elections, the revelations merely accelerated a longer-term trend in public policy towards modest individual donor limits, party spending limits, restrictions on corporate and union giving, the use of public funds or tax credits to subsidize party activities and limits on the role of third-party advertising during elections.

Political fund-raising in Canada was unregulated until the mid-1970s, and fell into disrepute after scandals involving corporate influence over Liberal campaigns. But the 1974 Election Expenses Act imposed rules on the raising and spending of political funding. The ensuing decades saw the propagation of election-financing laws at both the federal and provincial levels that reflected similar principles, chief among them the notion that public funding of parties blunts the reliance on significant amounts of cash from corporations or unions.

Perhaps the starkest contrast between Canada and the United States, however, involves third-party advertising during elections. The *Citizens United* decision, which assigned freedom of expression rights to corporations, essentially removed all limits on third-party advertising. In Quebec, separatist governments imposed strict exclusions for this kind of advertising during referendum campaigns (a restriction that fed the sponsorship scandal). While federal election laws also had limits on third-party advertising, in 2000, the National Citizens Coalition—a right-of-centre advocacy group run at the time by one Stephen Harper—challenged the constitutionality of those rules, including a $150,000 spending limit and disclosure requirements (in other words, the sponsors of the ad had to identify themselves).

The Supreme Court in 2000 partially agreed with the NCC and struck down some of the provisions challenged by them, but they left many others in place, including, critically, the disclosure rule. In contrast to *Citizens United*, the Canadian Supreme Court's ruling isn't rooted in legal arguments about whether organizations enjoy free speech rights; even if they did, they would be subject to the Charter of Rights' "reasonable limits" test. It's also worth noting that, as with other contentious issues, like abortion, there's been no relitigating of that judgment or efforts by Parliament to change these rules. Canadian law on third-party advertising and the transparency provisions in the election laws is effectively settled.

None of this is to say that Canadian politics is squeaky clean. The extensive corruption scandals in the Quebec construction industry attest to the way politicians can use public sector contracts to reward their friends. But these stories remain on the other side of the legal line dictating what's acceptable in terms of buying influence. And there's plenty of evidence of a national, nonpartisan consensus about limiting the influence of money from vested interests on elections and parties.

As for gerrymandering, the problem is virtually nonexistent in Canada because riding boundaries are set by arm's length bodies whose expert members draw on census data and public consultation processes. The most contentious points about federal election districts has to do with the number of voters in average rural ridings relative to far more populous urban ones. The Supreme Court has upheld population skews that have been criticized for giving rural MPs too much clout at the expense of large urban areas, which produce more wealth but have more complex needs from the point of view of the provision of public services.

IT'S TRUE THAT Canadian democratic institutions are threatened by the long-term decline in voter participation based on demographics. And although Canada leads the world in the proportion of immigrants who become citizens, recent declines in naturalization are also troubling. The trend may reflect the fact that the financial requirements to acquire citizenship are too steep or that the language competency standards have become too difficult for some newcomers.

At the same time, Canadian voters still take a more engaged and positive view of electoral politics and central government than Americans, many of whom have come to regard public services and federal institutions as hopelessly corrupt and inefficient— hardly a surprise when voters are carpet-bombed by televised attack ads at election time.

U.S. and Canadian attitudes towards democracy and governance bear out this long-term divergence in outlooks. While citizens of both countries have similarly respectful feelings about their armed forces, Canadian trust in institutions like the judiciary or legislative bodies is now running almost twice as high as Americans' sentiments. Public confidence in Canadian elections also surged between 2014 and 2017, offering yet another explanation of why Trudeau backed away from icing first-past-the-post elections. By contrast, barely half of Americans are satisfied with their democracy, a statistic that hardly bodes well in a country that boasts about its role as a global paragon of democracy and freedom.

There are other diverging indicators as well. The Democrats and Republicans have taken turns holding the White House, but the proportion of Americans whose vote is up for grabs has shrunk dramatically as the electorate grows more polarized. Canadian elections produce a wide spectrum of results—majorities; minorities; unexpected regional turnovers; parties that emerge, soar and dwindle or merge with others. In the past three decades, both the Tories and the Liberals have experienced dramatic victories and humiliating losses that required them to spend years rebuilding themselves. It is a highly dynamic political arena.

It is also an increasingly representative one. Women make up 26 per cent of the House of Commons and half the Trudeau cabinet. By contrast, women (as of 2017) accounted for 19.4 per cent of the seats in the U.S. House of Representatives, a fifth in the Senate and only two of Trump's fifteen-member cabinet. In the British Parliament, women (including Prime Minister Theresa May) held 29 per cent of seats prior to the June 2017 snap election, a record high.

As for immigrants and minorities, I'm not aware of another country where 13 per cent of representatives in the national legislature were born outside the country: 46 of the 338 MPs elected in 2015. In addition, 13.6 per cent are visible minorities whose families came from all over the world and another 3 per cent (10 MPs) are Indigenous Canadians. The Trudeau cabinet, as of 2017, also includes former refugees Maryam Monsef (Afghanistan via Iran) and Ahmed Hussen (Somalia), the minister of immigration and citizenship. Visible minorities and newcomers, moreover, are regularly elected to other parties, including the Tories and even the Bloc Québécois, which seems a bit ironic, considering the latter's commitment to breaking up the country.

These proportions, though historic, still lag slightly behind Canadian demographic trends at large. As of 2016, immigrants accounted for 22 per cent of Canada's total population (although many are not yet eligible to vote), while 20 per cent of Canadian residents were visible minorities.

On this measure of democratic robustness, Canada also seems to outpace the U.S. It's true that there's been a steady increase in minority representation at the federal level in the U.S. The 114th Congress, elected in the 2014 midterm races, was the most diverse ever, with nonwhites accounting for 17 per cent of all members of the House and Senate. Still, as the Pew Research Center points out, that historic result falls well short of American demographics: nonwhites account for 38 per cent of the U.S. population. The differential is 21 per cent, compared to 6 per cent in Canada.[7]

When we look at all these comparisons, it's easy to see a virtuous circle at work in Canada and a vicious cycle playing out in the U.S. As Canada has become increasingly diverse, its overall acceptance of immigration and cultural differences has grown, and that steady long-term shift in public opinion and values has solidified into a broad consensus about the role that newcomers play. While poverty is relatively high compared to Europe's social democratic paradises, so is social and economic mobility.

Well before Sadiq Khan became the mayor of London, England, in 2016, Calgary's Naheed Nenshi became the first Muslim (he's Is-

maili) elected to lead a large North American city; identity politics
played no discernible role in his victory—a charismatic business
professor, Nenshi credited his reformist victory to Calgary's increasingly cosmopolitan, global outlook. The growing diversity in
the House of Commons is more than just a compelling indicator of
social mobility and the relative dynamism of Canada's democratic
institutions. Rather, those results solidify a recognition among all
parties that the road to victory in Canada in the twenty-first century runs through hundreds of ethnically diverse urban and suburban neighbourhoods, whose residents probably benefited—either
directly, indirectly or generationally—from policies and public institutions designed to integrate newcomers.

Indeed, as Harper discovered during his party's drubbing in
2015, those voters may have socially conservative attitudes on some
moral and economic issues. However, they definitely will not be
impressed by politicians blowing the sorts of dog whistles that allowed Trump to mobilize so much racial resentment in 2016.

Conclusion

Months before Donald Trump won the Republican nomination and then the U.S. presidency, Matthew MacWilliams, a University of Massachusetts postdoctoral candidate, stumbled across a striking way of looking at a candidate who seemed to defy all the rules of politics.[1]

His polling research had revealed that parenting styles were a powerful predictor of voter attitudes towards Trump. In particular, MacWilliams discovered that those who preferred authoritarian child-rearing approaches—who valued traits such as obedience and good behaviour in their children over curiosity or independence—were much more likely to back Trump. Moreover, their support wasn't strictly contingent on traditional party preferences. As MacWilliams's polls showed, authoritarian parenting preferences can be found among both Republicans and Democrats.

To further confirm his hypothesis, he also looked at correlations between those with authoritarian outlooks and more specific political views, such as attitudes towards the protection of minorities, terrorism and immigration. The results further confirmed the distinct alignment of values and politics that allowed

Trump to win over working-class Midwesterners, religious South-erners and even some affluent younger people, among them voters who might have balked at his positions on LBGTQ+ rights or looked askance at his behaviour.

Upon taking office, the contrast between President Trump and Prime Minister Justin Trudeau came into stark relief. The two men offer vivid—even startling—opposites in terms of the way they present their masculinity. Trump is status obsessed, dominant in voice and manner, bullying and narcissistic. He boasted during the campaign about sexually assaulting women and made not-so-subtle allusions to his prowess in bed. Trudeau offers a metrosexual public persona—trim and handsome but courteous, attentive, upbeat and conspicuous in his assertions about gender equality. It's little won-der that Trudeau and Barack Obama got along so well—in every way, the forty-fourth president and the forty-fifth could scarcely be more different, not just politically and intellectually but also in the way they present themselves as men.

These three leaders are unique individuals, of course. But they express—and reflect—something important about the values of the societies that produced them. This, indeed, is one of the most obvi-ous conclusions from the analysis of the evolving American and Ca-nadian social values that Environics has been tracking since 1992.

Our research has looked at a broad range of attitudes—every-thing from outlooks on advertising and consumption to violence, authority and nontraditional families. Anticipating MacWilliams's findings, we have long tracked attitudes towards the role of the fa-ther in American and Canadian families, and the results tell an im-portant tale about why these two countries are on diverging paths despite a common border and extensive trade ties.

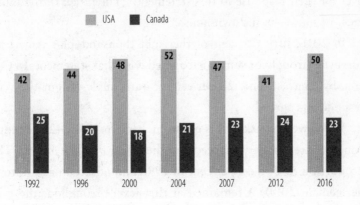

Agree: Father of the family must be master in his own house
1992 – 2016 Canada and USA

USA ▪ Canada

Environics Social Values Survey (2016)

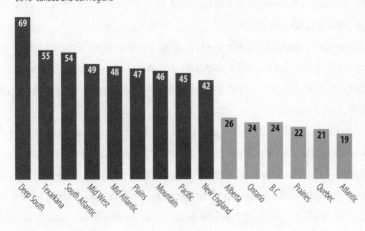

Agree: Father of the family must be master in his own house
2016 Canada and USA regions

Environics Social Values Survey (2016)

In order to understand the orientation to the structure of authority in the family in each country, we asked those age fifteen and over for their response to this statement: "The father of the family must be master in his own house."

In 2016, fifty per cent of the eight thousand–plus Americans surveyed strongly or somewhat agreed with that statement. In Canada, by contrast, only 23 per cent of our sample of four thousand respondents agreed.

When we first asked this question, back in 1992, 42 per cent of American respondents agreed that the father must be master. That proportion rose to 44 per cent in 1996 and nosed up again, to 48 per cent in 2000. It remained at that level throughout the post-9/11 George W. Bush years, and then declined somewhat during the Obama era to 41 per cent in 2012. However, as American Republicans and Democrats were in the process of selecting Donald Trump and Hillary Clinton as their presidential candidates, the proportion of Americans who said the father must be the master reached a historic high.

No one should be surprised that support for Donald Trump is highly correlated with support for patriarchy, and, conversely, support for gender equality is highly correlated with support for Hillary Clinton.

And Canada? The proportion of patriarchy supporters has been hovering in the low 20s, despite the influx of migrants from countries with more traditional attitudes about gender roles (35 per cent of self-identified immigrants believe Dad should be on top) as well as a mild backlash against feminism among Gen X and Y men (aged twenty-five to forty-four). In the U.S., 56 per cent of immigrants opt for patriarchy in the home.

In the Deep South (Tennessee, Alabama, Mississippi), 69 per cent now believe the father must be master; in New England, the figure is only 42 per cent, and all other regions fall somewhere in between.

It's worth noting that in Canada, there is far less variation in prevailing regional attitudes about patriarchy. The proportions range from a high of 26 per cent in Alberta, to a low of 18 per cent in Atlantic Canada. What's impossible to ignore is that Canada's most patriarchal province—Alberta, a place Canadians most likely associate with hard-driving social conservatism, pickup trucks and the frontier mentality—is still significantly less patriarchal than the least patriarchal region of the U.S.

If we dig even deeper into the demographics, we see some other telling patterns. Sixty per cent of American men think Father must be master at home compared to 41 per cent of American women. In Canada, 31 per cent of men think Dad should be boss, and the proportion among women is just 16 per cent.

I dwell on patriarchy as a social value because it is so meaningful in terms of the way we organize and govern our societies. It shouldn't be a surprise that in a country where patriarchal values continue to be so dominant, there's virtually no maternity leave, reproductive rights remain deeply contentious, and health care is heavily dependent on employment status.

Our surveys show that patriarchy is also highly correlated with religiosity, parochialism, xenophobia, patriotism, gun ownership and support for the death penalty—all positions prevalent in the so-called red states. Americans also tend to be far more religious than Canadians (and indeed most other industrialized nations). Canadians, in turn, are more accepting of nontraditional families and marriage outside one's group. Americans are more pessimistic about the direction of their country, whereas Canadians tend to be satisfied.

American society is famously polarized: a 50–50 nation with an increasingly tribal two-party system, red and blue bitterly divided on a host of issues large and small. The fact that half of Americans remain devoted to patriarchal authority in the home while the other half is unwilling to automatically defer to Dad is like a powerful tectonic fault line that impacts the country's entire social and political life.

There's another intriguing contrast that shines light on why partisan polarization characterizes the politics of one country and not the other. In Environics's Focus 2011 survey, we asked respondents for their views on compromise. Attitudes on this subject, we thought, would reveal something important about how communities and elected officials address difficult and divisive subjects. The results were revealing: 58 per cent of Canadians said they preferred elected officials who make compromises with their adversaries, whereas only 40 per cent of Americans took this stance. Similarly, 54 per cent of Americans reported that they like elected officials who stick to their positions, while only 38 per cent of Canadians do.

In one country, "compromise" is a dirty word; in the other, it's an expectation about the right way to conduct the public's business. This glimpse into the two countries' political cultures goes some distance towards explaining the partisan gridlock that gripped the U.S. Congress for much of Barack Obama's term. It also explains the difficulty Republicans of various stripes have had when they were confronted with decisions such as repealing Obamacare and approving tax and spending measures proposed by a Republican president.

. . . .

WE BEGAN TRACKING more than fifty social values on both sides of the 49th parallel in the aftermath of the 1988 federal election, during which the proposed Canada-U.S. free trade agreement was the dominant issue. The Liberals, then led by John Turner, memorably ran against the deal, using a highly effective ad showing someone removing the border on a map with a pencil eraser.

Critics of the agreement, mostly those on the centre-left, warned that by opening the borders and ceding decision making over trade disputes to an unelected tribunal, Canadian governments would be forced to relinquish the policies that made the country different than that of our neighbours. Health care, labour laws, economic development policies—all of these would have to be negotiated away as we sought to compete with a trading partner ten times our size. Or so went the argument, which was reprised in 1992 with discussions about the wider North American agreement, NAFTA, that included Mexico.

Economic pressure to align national policies would also lead to a convergence of values: these deals, some people warned, would inevitably make Canadians more like Americans. Indeed, there was a time when many informed Canadians felt the values of the two countries were growing more and more similar, and that the only real differences were between the Deep South and Quebec. Yes, our histories—revolution and the pursuit of life, liberty and happiness versus a negotiated divorce, or, more accurately, a move to separate bedrooms in the same royal household, in the name of peace, order and good government—were very different. But in the age of mass communications and consumption of mass-produced consumer goods, the differences would inevitably fade.

Yet something unexpected has occurred in the twenty-first century. When it comes to the value dimension of patriarchy, these generalizations do not stand up to evidence gathered broadly over a long period.

In 2002, EKOS asked Canadians if Canada was becoming more or less like the U.S. Fifteen years ago, 58 per cent said we were becoming more like the U.S. and only 9 per cent less like the republic. In the spring of 2017, we repeated this question in a national survey and found a change of opinion: today, only 27 per cent of us think Canada is becoming more like the U.S. and a nearly equal 26 per cent say we are, in fact, becoming less and less like our fractious southern neighbour.

As we've seen, one of the ways this difference has expressed itself is a rejection of the sort of politics that brought Trump to office, informed Brexit and contributed to the relative electoral success of the likes of Marine Le Pen. But on an even deeper level, our values tracking shows a long-term shift among Canadians towards a more global and tolerant outlook, as well as a rejection of the politics of division—something Stephen Harper learned the hard way.

I'm not suggesting that Canada has coasted into some kind of a postpartisan nirvana of open-mindedness about the sorts of issues that perennially divide Americans, or at least enough Americans to allow those disputes to keep burning. Nor can we say with certainty that angry populism won't rear its head—or be more effectively channeled by a particularly charismatic leader—at some future date.

What is true, however, is that Canada has long witnessed populist eruptions, on both the right and the left—western Progressives rising up to express agrarian discontent against eastern moneyed elites, Tommy Douglas's Cooperative Commonwealth Federation, Alberta's Social Credit Party, Quebec's Créditistes.

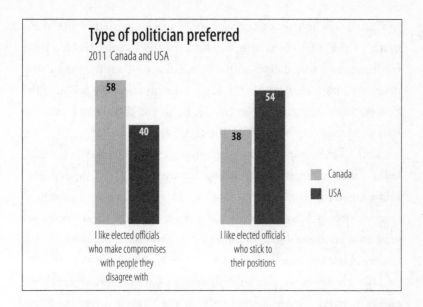

In the postwar era, the western/rural backlash against bilingual-ism and the efforts to keep Quebec from seceding found expression in Preston Manning's Reform Party. In Quebec, populist nation-alism produced the Parti Québécois and then the Bloc Québécois after the failure of the Meech Lake and Charlottetown constitu-tional accords, and later drove the rise and fall of the xenophobic ADQ in the late 2000's and the Parti Quebecois Charter of Values.

The Harper government anted up the most recent version of back-lash with its "tough on crime" laws, the so-called barbaric cultural practices snitch line, and the largely theatrical fight (few doubted that the courts would call the move unconstitutional) to force Muslim women who wear niqabs to show their faces at citizenship ceremonies.

As Memorial University political scientist Alex Marland, a brand expert, pointed out in *The Globe and Mail*, the federal Liberals have been the party of national unity whose single pre-occupation after Quebec's Quiet Revolution was to keep Quebec in Canada. When that issue was more or less settled in the aftermath of the 1995 referendum, the Liberals had to replace their traditional raison d'être with the ideology of multiculturalism, diversity and inclusion. Pierre Trudeau embodied the spirit of the first national vision; his son Justin, he of the diverse and gender-balanced cabinet, exemplifies the second.

Both of these aspirational ideologies generated backlashes, which led to Liberal defeats, most successfully with Harper's Conservatives (2006 to 2015). For most of that time, Harper was astute enough to give his backlash base enough red meat to assuage those voters yet wise enough to reach out to immigrants and visible minorities living in the suburbs of major cities, appealing where possible to their more socially conservative patriarchal values. But the moment Harper chose to pander more aggressively to the Conservatives' backlash base, he lost crucial support in the multicultural suburbs, support that cost the Conservatives an election they might have won.

As we have seen, there is plenty of polling evidence to show that the majority of Canadians today embrace gender, racial, ethnic, religious equality and LGBTQ+ rights. We also see concerns among the majority (albeit a declining one) that immigrants are not integrating quickly enough into mainstream Canadian society, although that society itself is changing constantly to reflect the cultures and values of new arrivals.

Indeed, just as bilingualism and the efforts to accommodate Quebec nationalism spawned a political backlash, it seems inevitable that the ideology of cultural diversity will produce its own backlash. Throughout the Conservative leadership campaign, polls consistently showed support for Kellie Leitch's notion of a Canadian values test, a signal that there are political dividends to harvest by appealing to the more fearful angels of our nature.

That she was also ridiculed and ultimately unsuccessful revealed something about the location of the boundaries of acceptable political discourse in Canada and offers a precise answer to the question of whether "it" could happen here.

We don't want to fight to see who is right. We want to talk and talk, to see who can stay awake long enough to have the last word. Toronto had its moment with Rob Ford; the Parti Québécois thought it had the winning ticket with its Charter of Values. Alberta's rural social conservatives thought they'd regain power with the Wildrose Party. But in each case, Canadians found the centre. With four in ten of us foreign born or second generation, and with most projected population growth coming from immigration, our ever-changing demography has become not only our defining feature but also the engine that injects values of openness, tolerance and compromise into every sphere of social life.

Could Canadians suddenly find themselves seized by the rage-fueled politics of exclusion and enthralled by a tough-guy autocrat? I suppose anything is possible. But if we go beyond the fleeting politics of the day and look more closely at those underlying values, the answer becomes clear: we've had our flings with polarizing populists, but when the buzz wears off, we always seem to muddle our way back to the middle.

Acknowledgements

This book, like the others I have managed to produce, is the product of a team effort. Such is survey research. Advanced data analysis was performed by Dr. David Jamieson, Environics Research Group's chief scientist. Demographic data was provided by Dr. Doug Norris, the chief demographer at Environics Analytics. Both are the best in their field. Expert counsel and access to the Focus Canada archive was provided by my supremely professional colleague Dr. Keith Neuman, the executive director of the Environics Institute for Survey Research, which I founded in 2006.

Working closely with me in crafting the words that expressed our findings and putting them into the larger sociohistorical context was the estimable writer John Lorinc; my long-time colleague Amy Langstaff also contributed. Both of these writers are brilliant and very skilled at what they do.

While the evening of November 8, 2016, the night of the improbable election of Donald Trump to the U.S. presidency, may have inspired this book, it would not have happened without the encouragement of my agent of nearly twenty years, the redoubtable

Bruce Westwood, and of course without the support of Kevin Hanson, the publisher of Simon & Schuster. The remarkable Brendan May served as S&S's astute editor, shepherding this book from inspiration to production in record speed.

To all I owe my deepest thanks.

A Note on Sources

Unless otherwise noted, the survey findings described in this book come from research conducted by Environics Research Group or by the Environics Institute for Survey Research and are used with permission of the company or Institute. The research programs the book draws on most often are:

Focus Canada began as a syndicated research program, and was conducted by Environics Research Group on a quarterly basis without interruption from 1976 through 2009. In 2010, Focus Canada was taken up by the nonprofit Environics Institute as a public interest research project that includes an ongoing series of surveys to continue tracking Canadian public opinion on various public policy and social issues facing the country (e.g., economy, health care, multiculturalism, crime and justice, Canada's role in the world). Focus Canada findings are available free at the web address below; individual reports state field dates, sample sizes and other methodological information (www.environicsinstitute.org/institute-projects/current-projects/focus-canada).

Environics Social Values surveys have been conducted almost annually in Canada since 1983, and roughly every four years in the

United States since 1992. The Environics social values measurement system seeks to understand the structure of social values in society and monitor changes in those values over time. Further information about the Environics Social Values research program is available at http://environicsresearch.com/what-are-social-values/.

Notes

INTRODUCTION: COULD IT HAPPEN HERE?

1. "Hon. Kellie Leitch Unveils Muslim Snitch Line for Barbaric Cultural Practices Tip Line Hotline," YouTube, www.youtube.com/watch?v=4msHDzO-GQ4.
2. Bill S-7 (Historical): Zero Tolerance for Barbaric Cultural Practices Act, https://openparliament.ca/bills/41-2/S-7/.
3. CBC News, "Niqab Ban for Public Servants Would Be Considered: Stephen Harper," October 6, 2015, www.cbc.ca/news/politics/stephen-harper-niqab-ban-public-servants-1.3258943.
4. "An Act to Amend the Citizenship Act and to Make Consequential Amendments to Other Acts," Government of Canada, http://lois-laws.justice.gc.ca/eng/AnnualStatutes/2014_22/page-1.html.
5. Canadian Federal Election, 2011, Wikipedia, https://upload.wikimedia.org/wikipedia/commons/9/92/%C3%89lection-f%C3%A9d%C3%A9rale-canadienne-2011.png.
6. Rachel Surman, "A Snapshot of Toronto: 51% of Residents Were Born Outside Canada, Vital Signs Report Finds," October 7, 2014, http://news.nationalpost.com/toronto/a-snapshot-of-toronto-51-of-residents-were-born-outside-canada-vital-signs-report-finds; "Toronto the Diverse: BBC Study Declares City Most Diverse in the World," University of Toronto, May 16, 2016, https://media.utoronto.ca/u-of-t-in-the-news/toronto-the-diverse-bbc-study-declares-city-most-diverse-in-the-world/.
7. "Foreign Born Population of the United Kingdom," Wikipedia, https://en.wikipedia.org/wiki/Foreign-born_population_of_the_United_Kingdom.

8. Cited in CBC News, "Conservative Party Officials Get Scathing Review of 2015 Election Campaign," www.cbc.ca/news/politics/conservative-election -post-mortem-vancouver-1.3604938.

9. Robert Brym, "Immigration and the Future of Canadian Society: An Introduction," Proceedings of the Second S. D. Clark Symposium on the Future of Canadian Society (Oakville, 2017), p. 7.

10. Faith Goldy, "Scholarships for Refugees, Not Whites," The Rebel, March 4, 2017, www.therebel.media/scholarships_for_refugees_not_whites.

11. Michael Valpy, "Populist Anger Is Real, and Canada Had Better Wake Up," The Globe and Mail, March 13, 2017, www.theglobeandmail.com/opinion/ populist-anger-is-real-and-canada-had-better-wake-up/article34268031/.

12. Zack Taylor, "Who Elected Rob Ford, and Why? An Ecological Analysis of the 2010 Toronto Election," paper presented at the Canadian Political Science Association conference, Waterloo, Ontario, May 2011, www.cpsa-acsp.ca/ papers-2011/Taylor.pdf.

13. Brexit poll tracker, Financial Times, https://ig.ft.com/sites/brexit-polling/.

14. The Economist, Brexit poll tracker, www.economist.com/blogs/graphicdetail /2016/06/britain-s-eu-referendum.

15. Jill Slattery, "1 in 6 Canadians Support Donald Trump for President," Vancity Buzz, September 2, 2015, www.vancitybuzz.com/2015/09/donald-trump- canada-insights-west-poll.

16. Alicja Siekierska, "Majority of Voters Think Trump Would Be Bad for Canada, Poll Says," Toronto Star, November 12, 2016, www.thestar.com/news/canada /2016/11/12/majority-of-voters-think-trump-would-be-bad-for-canada-poll- says.html.

17. John Helliwell, Richard Layard, and Jeffrey Sachs, World Happiness Report 2016 (New York: Sustainable Development Solutions Network, 2016), http:// worldhappiness.report/wp-content/uploads/sites/2/2016/03/HR-V1_web.pdf.

CHAPTER ONE: THE GLOBAL RE-AWAKENING OF XENOPHOBIC POPULISM

1. D. Wang, "U.S.-China Trade, 1971–2012: Insights into the U.S.-China Relationship," Asia-Pacific Journal 11, no. 4 (June 16, 2013), http://apjjf.org /2013/11/24/Dong-Wang/3958/article.html.

2. "U.K. Public Opinion over Immigration: Overall Attitudes and Levels of Concern," Migration Observatory, University of Oxford, November 29, 2016, www.migrationobservatory.ox.ac.uk/resources/briefings/uk-public-opinion- toward-immigration-overall-attitudes-and-level-of-concern/.

3. Ronald Inglehart and Pippa Norris, "Trump, Brexit, and the Rise of Populism: Economic Have-Nots and Cultural Backlash," working paper, Harvard Kennedy School, July 2016.

4. Anthony Heath and Lindsay Richards, "Attitudes Towards Immigration and Their Antecedents: Topline Results from Round 7 of the European Social Survey" (London: Centre for Comparative Social Surveys, 2016), www.europeansocialsurvey.org/docs/findings/ESS7_toplines_issue_7 _immigration.pdf.

5. James Traub, "The Party That Wants to Make Poland Great Again," *New York Times*, November 2, 2016, www.nytimes.com/2016/11/06/magazine/the-party-that-wants-to-make-poland-great-again.html?_r=0.

6. "Wikipedia Blocked in Turkey," Associated Press, April 29, 2107, www.cbc.ca/ news/world/wikipedia-blocked-in-turkey-1.4091913.

7. Martijn Lampert and Anne Blanksma Çeta, "Why Elites Are Failing . . . and People Revolt" (Amsterdam: Glocalities, 2017).

8. Thomas Huddleston, Ozge Bilgill, Anne-Linde Joki, and Zvezda Vankova, Migrant Integration Policy Index 2015, www.mipex.eu/key-findings.

9. Ibid. The MIPEX rankings evaluate 167 policy indicators in areas such as labour market mobility, family reunion policies, education, political participation, access to citizenship and anti-discrimination policies. In 2014, the most recent version, Canada ranked first on the anti-discrimination metric, with a score of 92 out of 100; fifth for labour mobility, and fourth for education.

10. Doug Saunders, "Marine Le Pen's National Front: Old Brand, New Spin," *The Globe and Mail*, April 21, 2017, www.theglobeandmail.com/opinion/marine-le-pen-old-brand-new-spin/article34774469/.

11. Ibid.

12. Ibid.

13. John Berry, "Multiculturalism: Psychological Perspectives," in *The Multiculturalism Question: Debating Identity in 21st-Century Canada*, ed. Jack Jedwab (Montreal: McGill-Queen's University Press, 2014).

14. "Obama Averages 47.9% Job Approval as President," Gallup, January 20, 2017, www.gallup.com/poll/202742/obama-averages-job-approval-president. aspx.

15. Derek Thompson, "Who Are Donald Trump's Supporters, Really?" *The Atlantic*, March 1, 2016, www.theatlantic.com/politics/archive/2016/03/who-are-donald-trumps-supporters-really/471714/.

16. "The American Identity: Points of Pride, Conflicting Views, and a Distinct Culture," Associated Press–NORC Center for Public Affairs Research, 2016, http://apnorc.org/projects/Pages/HTML%20Reports/points-of-pride-conflicting-views-and-a-distinct-culture.aspx.

17. Ibid. Two-thirds of Democrats believe that the mixing of cultures and values from around the world is very or extremely important to American identity,

whereas just 35 per cent of Republicans express the same belief. But when asked about the significance of a culture grounded in Christian religious beliefs, the result is almost exactly opposite.

CHAPTER TWO: WE'VE BEEN HERE BEFORE

1. Richard J. Brennan, "Even One Dissenting Canadian Enough to Kill Long-form Census, Says Clement," *Toronto Star*, October 6, 2010, www.thestar .com/news/canada/2010/10/06/even_one_dissenting_canadian_enough_to_kill _longform_census_says_clement.html.

2. Anne Kingston, "Vanishing Canada: Why We're All Losers in Ottawa's War on Data," *Maclean's*, September 18, 2015, www.macleans.ca/news/canada/ vanishing-canada-why-were-all-losers-in-ottawas-war-on-data/.

3. Anthony Doob, "The Harper Revolution in Criminal Justice Policy . . . and What Comes Next," *Policy Options*, May 4, 2015, http://policyoptions.irpp .org/magazines/is-it-the-best-of-times-or-the-worst/doob-webster/.

4. "Canadians Support Long-form Census," Angus Reid Institute, July 22–23, 2010, http://angusreid.org/canadians_support_mandatory_long_form_census/.

5. Althia Raj, "Trudeau Liberals to Bring Back Mandatory Long-form Census," *Huffington Post*, November 5, 2015, www.huffingtonpost.ca/2015/11/05/ trudeau-census-long-form-navdeep-bains_n_8478692.html.

6. Jessica Glenza, "Donald Trump Retracts Call for Women Who Have Abortions to Be 'Punished,'" *The Guardian*, March 31, 2016, www.theguardian.com/ us-news/2016/mar/30/donald-trump-women-abortions-punishment.

7. Andrew Russell, "6 in 10 Canadians Support Abortion Under Any Circumstances: Ipsos Poll," Global News, http://globalnews.ca/news/2535846 /6-in-10-canadians-support-abortion-under-any-circumstances-ipsos-poll/.

8. Jeffrey Simpson, "Attacking the Supreme Court, the Conservatives Sink to a New Low," *Globe and Mail*, May 7, 2014, www.theglobeandmail.com/opinion /tories-sink-to-a-new-supreme/article18498810/.

9. "Canadian Confidence in Police, Courts Sees Significant Rebound over 2012 Sentiment," Angus Reid Global, May 6, 2014, http://angusreidglobal.com/wp-content/uploads/2014/05/ARG-Canadian-Perceptions-Police-Crime-2014.pdf.

10. *Canada (Attorney General) v. Bedford*, 2013, ruling available at www.canlii .org/en/ca/scc/doc/2013/2013scc72/2013scc72.html.

11. Laura Payton, "Prostitution Laws Could Be Changed Further Under Liberals," *Maclean's*, November 9, 2015, www.macleans.ca/politics/ottawa/prostitution-laws-could-see-more-changes-under-liberals/.

12. "(Understanding) Sex Work: A Health Research & Community Partnership," University of Victoria/Canadian Institute for Health Research, 2016, www .understandingsexwork.com/.

CHAPTER THREE: CANADA AND IMMIGRATION IN THE ERA OF TRUMP AND BREXIT

1. "The Last Liberals: Why Canada Is Still at Ease with Openness," *The Economist*, October 29, 2016, www.economist.com/news/briefing/21709291-why-canada-still-ease-openness-last-liberals.

2. Mike Maciag, "Analysis: Undocumented Immigrants Not Linked with Higher Crime Rates," *Governing*, March 2, 2017, www.governing.com/gov-data/safety-justice/undocumented-immigrants-crime-effects-study.html.

3. Christine Sismondo, "What the 'Yellow Peril' Tells Us About This Migrant Moment," *Maclean's*, March 19, 2017, www.macleans.ca/news/canada/what-canadas-yellow-peril-teaches-us-about-this-migrant-moment/.

4. "Canadian Immigration Policy," *Canadian Encyclopedia*, www.thecanadianencyclopedia.ca/en/article/immigration-policy/. Also "Canada: If You Build It, People Will Come," *Policy Options*, June 1, 2008, http://policyoptions.irpp.org/magazines/citizenship-and-immigration/canada-if-you-build-it-people-will-come/.

5. Li Xue and Li Xu, "An Educational Portrait of Postsecondary Educated Immigrants, 2006 Census," Immigration, Refugees and Citizenship Canada, 2010, www.cic.gc.ca/english/resources/research/education.asp.

CHAPTER FOUR: ON BEING MUSLIM IN CANADA—OPTIMISM WITH VIGILANCE

1. Aileen Donnelly and the Canadian Press, "Alan Kurdi's Father Blames Canada for Death of His Family as PM Suggests He Will Expedite Refugee Applications," *National Post*, September 10, 2015, http://news.nationalpost.com/news/canada/alan-kurdis-father-blames-canada-for-death-of-his-family-as-pm-suggests-he-will-expedite-refugee-applications.

2. After the election, almost two-thirds of Canadians supported the Liberals' promise to bring twenty-five thousand Syrian refugees to Canada. By contrast, just 28 per cent of Americans backed the Obama administration's plan to accept ten thousand Syrian refugees, with that figure rising to 39 per cent if Muslims claimants were excluded. *Committing Sociology*, p. 124.

3. "Zunera Ishaq, Who Challenged Ban on Niqab, Takes Citizenship Oath Wearing It," CBC News, October 5, 2015, www.cbc.ca/news/politics/zunera-ishaq-niqab-ban-citizenship-oath-1.3257762.

4. Katayoun Kishi, "Anti-Muslim Assaults Reach 9/11-era Levels, FBI Data Show," Pew Research, November 21, 2016, www.pewresearch.org/fact-tank/2016/11/21/anti-muslim-assaults-reach-911-era-levels-fbi-data-show/.

5. "SPLC Hatewatch Update: 1,094 Bias-Related Incidents in the Month Following the Election," Southern Poverty Law Center, December 16, 2016, www.splcenter.org/hatewatch/2016/12/16/update-1094-bias-related-incidents-month-following-election.

6. Caroline Alphonso, "Anti-Muslim Protesters Shout 'Hateful' Rhetoric at Toronto-area School Board Meeting," *Globe and Mail*, March 23, 2017, www.theglobeandmail.com/news/toronto/anti-muslim-protesters-descend-on-toronto-area-school-board-meeting/article34396168/?utm_source= Shared+Article+Sent+to+User&utm_medium=E-mail:+Newsletters+/+E-Blasts+/+etc.&utm_campaign=Shared+Web+Article+Links.

7. Alicja Siekierska, "Peel School Board Reaches out After Protester Ripped Qur'an," *Toronto Star*, March 29, 2017, www.thestar.com/news/gta/2017/03 /29/peel-school-board-reaches-out-after-protestor-ripped-quran.html.

8. Daniel LeBlanc, "Quebec City Mosque Shooter Was a 'Criminal Extremist': RCMP Commissioner," *Globe and Mail*, February 6, 2017, www .theglobeandmail.com/news/politics/quebec-city-mosque-shooter-was-a-criminal-extremist-rcmp-commissioner/article33920071/.

9. Kim Hjelmgaard, "Dutch Muslims Feel Anti-Islam Backlash in Liberal Holland," *USA Today*, March 9, 2017, www.usatoday.com/story/news/world /2017/03/09/netherlands-election-muslims-geert-wilders/98146882/.

10. Yoruk Bahceli, "Dutch Muslims Reflect on Geert Wilders Before Vote," Al Jazeera, March 14, 2017, www.aljazeera.com/indepth/features/2017/03/dutch-muslims-reflect-geert-wilders-vote-170313125601556.html.

11. "Quebec Town May Scrap Immigrant Code," the Canadian Press, May 10, 2010, www.cbc.ca/news/canada/montreal/quebec-town-may-scrap-immigrant-code-1.925377.

12. National Household Survey (NHS) Profile, 2011, Statistics Canada, *Canada (Code 01)* (table), Catalogue no. 99-004-XWE, Ottawa, released September 11, 2013, www12.statcan.gc.ca/nhs-enm/2011/dp-pd/prof/index.cfm?Lang=E.

13. Laila Kearney, "Nike to Launch High-tech Hijab for Female Muslim Athletes," Reuters, March 8, 2017, www.reuters.com/article/us-nike-hijab-idUSKBN16F2N1.

14. "Baltej Dhillon Case," Historica Canada, www.thecanadianencyclopedia.ca/en /article/baltej-dhillon-case/.

15. Kathleen Harris, "RCMP Allows Muslim Women Mounties to Wear Hijab," CBC News, August 24, 2016, www.cbc.ca/news/politics/rcmp-diversity-policy-hijab-1.3733829.

CHAPTER FIVE: THE TAXI DRIVER WITH THE PHD

1. Joe Friesen, "Despair and Frustration at Toronto's Jane and Finch," *Globe and Mail*, November 11, 2005, www.theglobeandmail.com/news/national/despair-and-frustration-at-torontos-jane-and-finch/article1130828/.

2. Richard Florida, "Look Out—Canada, Too, Could Catch the Riot Virus,"

Globe and Mail, August 19, 2011, www.theglobeandmail.com/opinion/look-out---canada-too-could-catch-the-riot-virus/article4192917/.

3. J. David Hulchanski, *The Three Cities Within Toronto: Income Polarization Among Toronto's Neighbourhoods, 1970–2000* (Toronto: University of Toronto Cities Centre, 2007), www.urbancentre.utoronto.ca/pdfs/curp/tnrn/Three-Cities-Within-Toronto-2010-Final.pdf.

4. Neighbourhood Change Research Partnership, Factor-Inwentash Faculty of Social Work, University of Toronto, 2011–17, http://neighbourhoodchange.ca/.

5. Hulchanski, *Three Cities Within Toronto*.

6. René Houle and Lahouaria Yssaad, "Recognition of Newcomers' Foreign Credentials and Work Experience," 2010, Statistics Canada, www.statcan.gc.ca/pub/75-001-x/2010109/article/11342-eng.htm.

7. Survey of Muslims in Canada, Environics Institute for Survey Research, 2016, www.environicsinstitute.org/uploads/institute-projects/survey%20of%20muslims%20in%20canada%202016%20-%20final%20report.pdf.

8. Rima Berns-McGown, "'I Am Canadian': Challenging Stereotypes About Young Somali Canadians," Institute for Research on Public Policy, January 15, 2013, http://irpp.org/research-studies/study-no38/.

9. Jill Grant, "Planning Responses to Gated Communities in Canada," paper presented at Gated Communities: Building Social Division or Safer Communities? conference, Glasgow, September 18–19, 2003, http://theoryandpractice.planning.dal.ca/_pdf/gated_communities/Grant_2003_planning_responses_Glasgow.pdf.

10. Deani Van Pelt, Jason Clemens, Brianna Brown, and Milagros Palacios, "Where Our Students Are Educated: Measuring Student Enrolment in Canada," Fraser Institute, 2015, www.fraserinstitute.org/studies/where-our-students-are-educated-measuring-student-enrolment-in-canada.

11. Enrolment trends, National Centre for Education Statistics, https://nces.ed.gov/fastfacts/display.asp?id=65.

12. Jed Kolko, "Where Private School Enrollment Is Highest and Lowest Across the U.S.," CityLab, August 13, 2014, www.citylab.com/housing/2014/08/where-private-school-enrollment-is-highest-and-lowest-across-the-us/375993/.

13. Charter schools, National Centre for Education Statistics, https://nces.ed.gov/fastfacts/display.asp?id=30.

14. National Centre for Education, Public charter school enrolment, 2017, Statistics, https://nces.ed.gov/programs/coe/indicator_cgb.asp.

15. Chris Li, "Canada's Private Colleges: The Lesser Known Players in Postsecondary Education," Statistics Canada, 2006, www.statcan.gc.ca/pub/11-621-m/11-621-m2006036-eng.htm.

16. Ou Lydia Liu, "Examining American Post-Secondary Education," Educational Testing Service research report, May 2011.

CHAPTER SIX: OCCUPY THIS—THE POLITICS OF INEQUALITY IN CANADA

1. Derek Thompson, "The Rise (and Rise and Rise) of the 0.01 Percent in America," *The Atlantic*, February 13, 2014, www.theatlantic.com/business/archive/2014/02/the-rise-and-rise-and-rise-of-the-001-percent-in-america/283793/.

2. Matthew Desmond, *Evicted: Poverty and Profit in the American City* (New York: Penguin Random House, 2016), www.evictedbook.com/.

3. Joshua Rothman, "The Lives of Poor White People," *New Yorker*, September 12, 2016, www.newyorker.com/culture/cultural-comment/the-lives-of-poor-white-people.

4. Environics Institute, "Income Inequality: What Does the Public See?" paper presented at the Canada 2020 Conference on Income Disparity and Polarization, 2012.

5. Middle Class Tax Cut, Liberal Party of Canada, www.liberal.ca/realchange/middle-class-tax-cut/.

6. Income Inequality, Conference Board of Canada, www.conferenceboard.ca/hcp/details/society/income-inequality.aspx.

7. OECD Forum 2015: Income Inequality in Figures, Organisation for Economic Co-operation and Development, www.oecd.org/forum/issues/oecd-forum-2015-income-inequality-in-figures.htm.

8. Raj Chetty, "Improving Opportunities for Economic Mobility: New Evidence and Policy Lessons," Federal Reserve Bank of St. Louis, 2016.

9. "Unionization Rates Falling," Statistics Canada, 2017, www.statcan.gc.ca/pub/11-630-x/11-630-x2015005-eng.htm.

10. "Trade Union Density," OECD.Stat, 2017, https://stats.oecd.org/Index.aspx?DataSetCode=UN_DEN.

11. "Overweight and Obesity Trends," National Institute of Diabetes and Digestive and Kidney Diseases, www.niddk.nih.gov/health-information/health-statistics/Pages/overweight-obesity-statistics.aspx#b.

12. "Infant, Child, and Teen Mortality," Child Trends Databank Indicator, 2016, www.childtrends.org/?indicators=infant-child-and-teen-mortality.

13. "Long-term Trends in Diabetes," Centers for Disease Control, Division of Diabetes Translation, April 2017, www.cdc.gov/diabetes/statistics/slides/long_term_trends.pdf.

14. Terrence McCoy, "Disabled, or Just Desperate?" *Washington Post*, March 30, 2017, www.washingtonpost.com/sf/local/2017/03/30/disabled-or-just-desperate/?utm_term=.fa307337630a.

15. Rob Stein, "Life Expectancy in U.S. Drops for First Time in Decades, Report Finds," NPR, December 8, 2016, www.npr.org/sections/health-shots/2016/12/08/504667607/life-expectancy-in-u-s-drops-for-first-time-in-decades-report-finds.

16. David U. Himmelstein, Steffie Woolhandler, Janis Sarra, Gordon Guyatt, "Health Issues and Health Care Expenses in Canadian Bankruptcies and Insolvencies," *International Journal of Health Services* 44, no. 1 (January 1, 2014): 7–23, www.ncbi.nlm.nih.gov/pubmed/24684082.

17. Kim LaCapria, "Money, Cash, Throes," Snopes, April 22, 2016, www.snopes.com/643000-bankruptcies-in-the-u-s-every-year-due-to-medical-bills/.

18. Samuel Osborne, "US Stress Levels Highest in 10 Years Following Donald Trump's Election Victory," *The Independent*, February 16, 2017, www.independent.co.uk/news/world/americas/us-politics/stress-levels-us-donald-trump-election-victory-united-states-psychologists-apa-study-research-a7584061.html.

19. "Perceived Life Stress," Statistics Canada, 2013, www.statcan.gc.ca/pub/82-625-x/2014001/article/14023-eng.htm.

20. See also Abraham Maslow, *A Theory of Human Motivation* (1943); Thorstein Veblen, *The Theory of the Leisure Class* (1899); Alain de Botton, *Status Anxiety* (2004).

CHAPTER SEVEN: DOING DEMOCRACY DIFFERENTLY?

1. The "World Values Surveys" were conducted in 2005–2007, and again in 2010–2014, www.worldvaluessurvey.org.

2. Roberto Stefan Foa and Yascha Mounk (2017), "The Signs of Deconsolidation," *Journal of Democracy* 27, no. 3 (July 2016): 5–17. www.journalofdemocracy.org/article/signs-deconsolidation.

3. Richard Wike, "4 Factors Driving Anti-establishment Sentiment in Europe," Pew Research, December 6, 2016, www.pewresearch.org/fact-tank/2016/12/06/4-factors-driving-anti-establishment-sentiment-in-europe/.

4. While the majority of the justices concluded that the absence of voter suppression measures proved that these protections were no longer necessary, the staunch liberal justice Ruth Bader Ginsburg wrote in her dissent that "[t]hrowing out [statutory protection] when it has worked and is continuing to work to stop discriminatory changes is like throwing away your umbrella in a rainstorm because you are not getting wet."

5. Elizabeth Kolbert, "Drawing the Line," *New Yorker*, June 27, 2016, www.newyorker.com/magazine/2016/06/27/ratfcked-the-influence-of-redistricting.

6. Drew DeSilver, "U.S. Trails Most Developed Countries in Voter Turnout," Pew

Research, May 15, 2017, www.pewresearch.org/fact-tank/2016/08/02/u-s-voter-turnout-trails-most-developed-countries/.

7. Jens Manuel Krogstad, "114th Congress Is Most Diverse Ever," Pew Research, January 12, 2015, www.pewresearch.org/fact-tank/2015/01/12/114th-congress-is-most-diverse-ever/.

CONCLUSION

1. Max Ehrenfreund, "A Strange but Accurate Predictor of Whether Someone Supports Donald Trump," *Washington Post*, February 1, 2016, www.washingtonpost.com/news/wonk/wp/2016/02/01/how-your-parenting-style-predicts-whether-you-support-donald-trump/?utm_term=.541f7b5cc882.

Index